Each pet is unique. Its appearance stems primarily from its *overall size*, the *shape of its body* and the *density and texture of the fur* combined with *the length of the coat*. The quality of bathing, drying and trimming will aid in different looks. Also, each stylist owns a unique set of knowledge and abilities. A highly knowledgeable stylist will be able to prioritize breed standard trimming techniques and apply them in a stylish manner. Learning the cuts is easy. Applying the trims to the wide variety of coat types can be the challenging part. However, with proper training and practice, all grooming jobs can become fun as well as routine, allowing you to sail through your day with the greatest of ease.

#1   GROOMING BODY STYLES

The five basic grooming styles performed over and over again in salons:

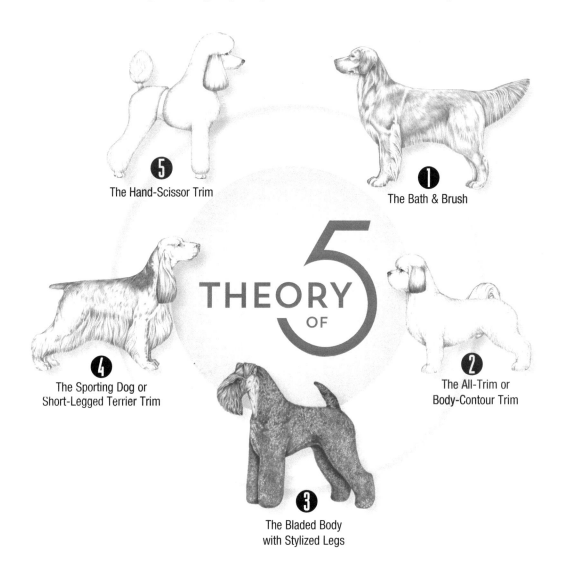

⑤ The Hand-Scissor Trim

① The Bath & Brush

THEORY OF 5

④ The Sporting Dog or Short-Legged Terrier Trim

② The All-Trim or Body-Contour Trim

③ The Bladed Body with Stylized Legs

The Bath & Brush

THE FOUNDATION FOR ALL

This is one of the most elementary jobs we do. The bath is the foundation for all other grooming. In a professional setting, this can be one of your most lucrative grooming jobs or the one that can cost you the most. It's critical to use time saving tools and techniques, especially on heavy coated dogs.

In many salons, the simple bath and brush grooming job can net up to 40–60 percent of the revenues for the entire business. There are a wide variety of dogs in this category, all based on the size of the pet, the density of the coat and the texture of the fur as well as its length.

Typical dogs and their coat types are:

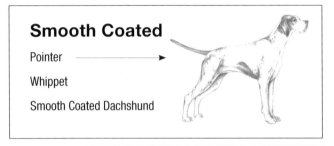

Smooth Coated

Pointer

Whippet

Smooth Coated Dachshund

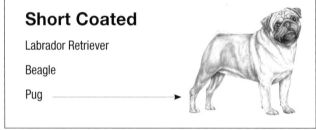

Short Coated

Labrador Retriever

Beagle

Pug

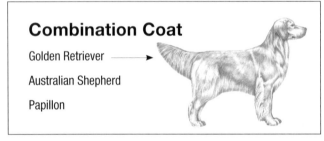

Combination Coat

Golden Retriever

Australian Shepherd

Papillon

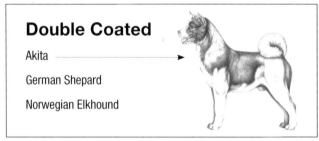

Double Coated

Akita

German Shepard

Norwegian Elkhound

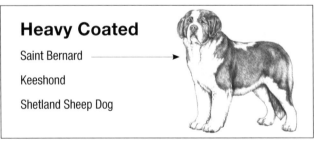

Heavy Coated

Saint Bernard

Keeshond

Shetland Sheep Dog

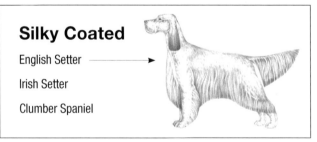

Silky Coated

English Setter

Irish Setter

Clumber Spaniel

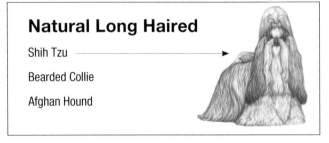

Natural Long Haired

Shih Tzu

Bearded Collie

Afghan Hound

So, what are your goals with this type of job?

First and foremost, you have to get the dog clean—**really clean**. The coat should feel squeaky clean to the touch when wet and super shiny when the coat is dry. If the coat is longer, it should flow and bounce as the dog moves. For curly coated dogs, the hair should look like a soft billowing cloud. All shedding coat should be removed along with all mats and tangles.

Bath and brush dogs should get only minor trimming to tidy them up. Areas that commonly need attention are the feet, though a few dogs need their ears tidied up. Dogs that normally get full haircuts—but are in for maintenance bathing between haircuts—may need their feet, face, ears and under the tail trimmed slightly.

The client has multiple choices: to use your grooming service, to use someone else's service or do it themselves. No matter how simple the job, if you want clients to return, it's essential you recognize and solve their problems. Even short coated dogs shed and can have a body odor problem, not to mention nails that need trimming and ears to be cleaned!

Clients bring their pets to a professional groomer for a variety of reasons, but it's always to solve a problem.

Typical reasons clients choose groomers are:

- Their pet smells
- The dog is dirty
- The coat is shedding
- The coat is tangled and or matted
- The nails need trimming
- The ears need cleaning
- The feet need minor trimming
- The client does not have the facility to bathe the pet at home
- The client does not have the tools
- The client does not want the mess at home

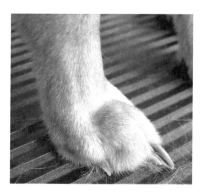

① ② ③ ④ ⑤

Our analysis of professionals who struggle with time management shows that in almost every case, ineffective bathing and drying methods are used. Regardless of the type of breed or coat you are working with, excellent bathing and drying skills are at the foundation of all grooming jobs and styles. So, how do you quickly and efficiently get a dog really clean? Here are some effective tips to help you do just that.

BATHING TIPS

- Use a high quality shampoo.

- When applying water or shampoo, let gravity do the work. Start on the top of the pet and work down.

- Shampoo twice—or three times if the coat is really dirty in areas.

❶ On short coated dogs, use a rubber curry to really work the lather down to the skin.

On heavy coated pets, use a high velocity dryer on them **before** the bath to lift the dirt and debris to the surface, allowing for better cleansing during the bath.

❷ On dogs with heavily soiled areas, use a scrub brush on feet, ears and under the tail area.

❸ In delicate areas, such as around the eyes, use a soft bristled toothbrush or a damp towel to help remove eye secretions.

❹ When rinsing, push the excessive shampoo and water from the coat by following behind the spray with your other hand— on larger dogs, use a tool such as the back side of plastic slicker brush or a sweat scraper typically used on horses. Keep the nozzle close to the skin.

❺ Don't forget to rinse the eyes with a gentle stream of lukewarm water to remove any traces of shampoo or debris from their eyes. Use caution not to let water go up their nose.

On the final rinse—rinse, rinse and rinse.

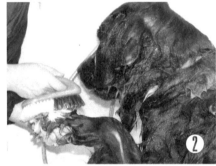

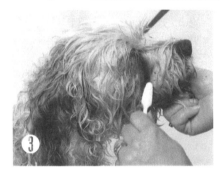

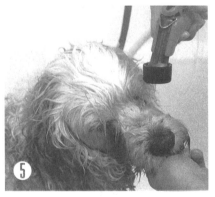

DRYING TIPS

- Thoroughly towel the pet dry before proceeding to an active drying method.

- Use the most powerful high velocity dryer available to you.

- Use a condenser cone with the high velocity dryer to remove as much excess moisture as possible.

❶ The initial pass with a high velocity dryer on heavy coated dogs often throws up quite a spray. Hold a towel behind the airflow to catch the spray so the pet will dry faster and nearby pets won't get a "shower."

❷ Keep the nozzle as close to the pet's skin as possible without causing "whip knots" (when the coat curls back on itself).

❸ Once the excessive moisture is removed, look for loose, shedding coat and focus on that area until shedding coat ceases to flow freely off the dog.

If there are mats or tangles in the coat, waggle the airflow back and forth a bit to loosen the tangle and create a coat pattern that resembles a spider web. Towards the end of the drying process, if there are still tangles or loose coat, give the area a light boost with a heavy slicker brush while drying to remove the last of the stubborn tangles.

❹ When the majority of moisture, loose coat and/or mats are removed from the coat, remove the condenser cone and hold the warm air flow close to the skin to speed drying and add body to the coat.

Use a consistent pattern while moving the high velocity airflow over the dog. On most pets, start at the base of the tail, moving up over the body, then down over the hips, shoulders, legs, feet, head and ears.

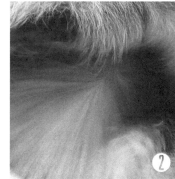

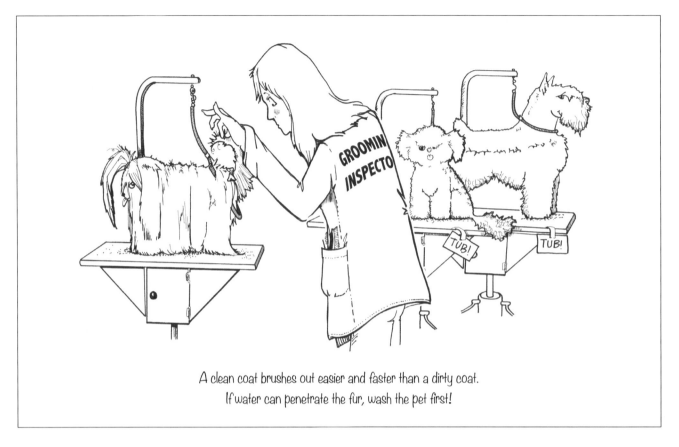

A clean coat brushes out easier and faster than a dirty coat.
If water can penetrate the fur, wash the pet first!

BRUSH OUT TIPS

- Let the high velocity dryer do most of the work for you when it comes to brushing and de-tangling. Air will never hurt the skin or coat of the dog.

- For pets that are heavily tangled or shedding, use the high velocity dryer in the tub while the pet is still lathered up. A large majority of the mats, tangles and shedding fur will slide out. It's the same concept as sliding a tight ring off a finger with soap and water. Plus, on shedding pets, the mess will be contained to the back wall of the tub and most of the shampoo will be blown off before the rinsing procedure.

- This method works great in mobile vans to save time and water with rinsing.

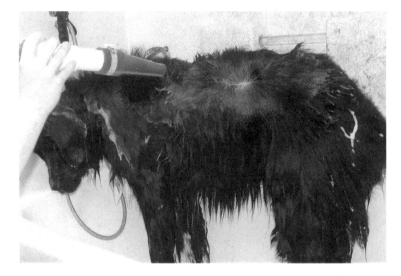

BRUSH OUT TIPS

  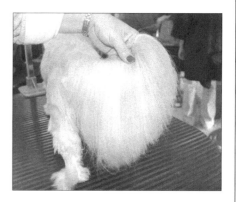

Once most of the mat, tangle or loose coat is "blown out," use a heavy slicker brush to "pat and pull" out the remaining coat or tangle.

Friction Areas

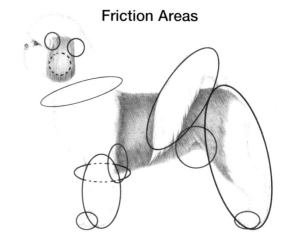

• Pay close attention to the "friction areas" for matting—behind ears, collar area, legs, arm pits, between toes, rear section and tail.

• Once the pet is dry, go over the entire pet again with a heavy brush and a wide-toothed comb.

• Check for damp spots, loose coat, tangles and coat density. Spend extra time in those areas with your tools, dryers and plain old-fashioned elbow grease.

• Thoroughly line brushing and combing ensures all tangles are removed all the way down to the skin.

TIPS FOR TIDYING UP THE BATH & BRUSH PET

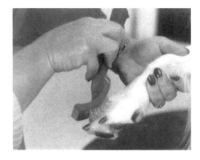

- On short coated dogs, one of the most effective and safe tools to remove loose coat is a rubber curry with larger flexible teeth shaped like upside down incense cones.

- Make sure feet are neatly trimmed and will stay that way for weeks. A heavy brush will effectively pull out loose and/or longer coat that needs to be trimmed and shaped.

- The ears should present a neat, trim outline. On natural ears needing a little help, use thinning shears around the outside edges to give a neat but natural appearance.

- On pets that normally get haircuts, but are in for a maintenance bath and brush in-between trims, the eye area, tummy and under the tail may need light trimming.

- Some clients like the entire "silhouette" of the pet's body outlined. Check with your client first and charge accordingly for the extra time spent on the pet. Scissors, combined with thinning shears, will give a nice, natural look.

Verify with new clients what is included in your "Bath & Brush." If they want more than the "normal," discuss the request, including such factors as safety for the pet, living environment and lifestyle as well as cost.

All-Trim or All-Over One-Length Trim

EXPOSING THE STRUCTURAL FEATURES OF THE DOG

This low maintenance trim style is highly popular with countless clients. This client is more concerned with an easy-to-care-for trim that minimizes hair care between grooming visits as well as the amount of dirt the pet brings into the home. This trim style also is well suited to pets that have a very low tolerance to the entire grooming process.

With this trim, accentuating the dog's best body features is not as important as smoothness and neatness. The body type and the structural features of the dog will come into full view—good or bad.

Almost any pet is a contender for this trim style:

Poodles

Golden Retrievers

Drop Coated Breeds (e.g. Lhasa Apso)

Labradors

Even Labradors or countless mixed breeds.

Cocker Spaniels

If the dog grows hair, it's a candidate for an "all trim."

...HOWEVER...

SOME DOGS JUST ARE NOT SUITED TO THIS STYLE.

They may either possess an unattractive body structure or
hair follicles that are prone to change with this trim style.

Many dogs from the sporting, terrier, working and herding groups have
harsh guard hairs that commonly are destroyed by clipper cutting. In
many cases, once the coat is trimmed, the harsh texture of such a coat
and its brilliant colors can be lost. Soft downy undercoat replaces the
harsh guard hairs. On many breeds, this soft coat is much lighter in
color, so when a dog is shaved the color can change dramatically.

On scores of double coated breeds, the fur often grows back much
thicker following a full shave off.

Dogs that were bred to perform active duties have coats that naturally
protect their skin and maintain a consistent body temperature. Dogs that
have had their coats artificially removed are prone to a number of health
issues, especially if they are active outdoor dogs. When freshly shaved, they
become prone to sunburn, insect bites and minor injuries caused by running
through underbrush or woods. Depending on the climate, overheating or
becoming chilled also are concerns.

This trim style, however, remains very popular with customers. For single coated
dogs that are indoors most of the time, this haircut style rarely poses health
concerns and is a great alternative for a low maintenance pet.

#1 GROOMING JOBS: ALL-TYPE TRIM OR BODY-CONTOUR TRIM

WHAT ARE YOUR GOALS WITH THIS TYPE OF JOB?

Smoothness and neatness are the only things going for this trim style. When trimming the coat, a maximum of three passes with the clipper is all that should be necessary to get the coat smooth—any more than that and you are not being resourceful with your clippers—less than that and you're being highly efficient. On some coats, going with the lay of the coat growth is the most efficient trimming method. On other dogs, cutting against the lay of the coat will be the fastest way to remove the hair.

TIPS FOR GETTING IT SMOOTH WITH SPEED AND EASE

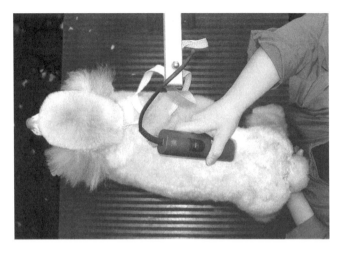
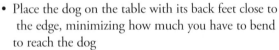

• Place the dog on the table with its back feet close to the edge, minimizing how much you have to bend to reach the dog

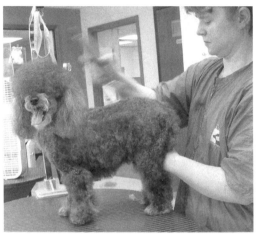

• Sometimes, the best way to do this is to have the pet stand across the table top.

• Keep the blade up on its "cutting edge" for optimum cutting action and safety. The shorter the cut, the higher the degree of tip.

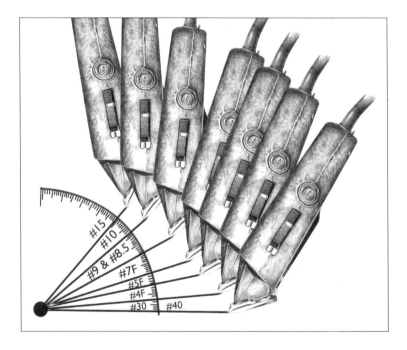

THEORY OF 5 — *Simplifying Pet Grooming Concepts for Everyday Pets ©2018*

TIPS FOR GETTING IT SMOOTH WITH SPEED AND EASE

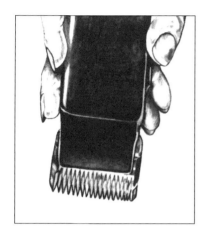
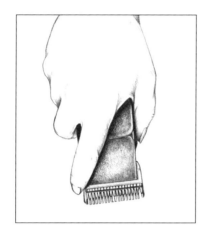
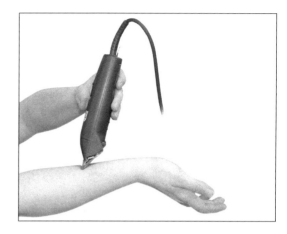

- Hold the clipper like a pencil for most of your trimming. Occasionally, you will need to use an over-handed hold on the clipper to maintain flexibility in your wrist.

- Maintain consistent clipper pressure as it contacts the skin. Use your own wrist or a partner's wrist as a gauge to test that you are applying consistent pressure.

- Always, always keep your wrist supple as you clipper the pet.

- For most trimming work, pull the clipper towards you, so your wrist remains supple.

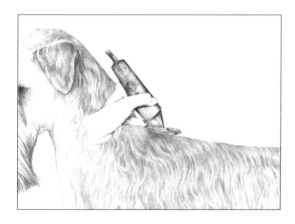
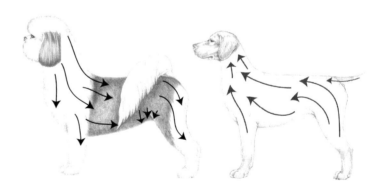

- For attach-on guard combs, rock the attach-on guard comb onto its heel, causing the tips of the teeth to rise slightly off the dog's skin as you make each clipper stroke.

- Clip with the natural lay of the coat, either with the grain or against the grain.

TIPS FOR GETTING IT SMOOTH WITH SPEED AND EASE

For coats that lay in a specific direction, selecting a blade two lengths longer than the desired trim length and used in reverse, can be highly effective. For example, when the job requires a #7F blade used with the lay of the coat, choose a #4F used in reverse. For the length of a #10 blade, use a #7F in reverse. This technique works well on such dogs as Cocker Spaniels, Schnauzers, Springers, Labs, Goldens and others with similar coats.

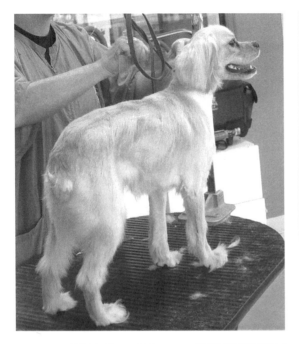

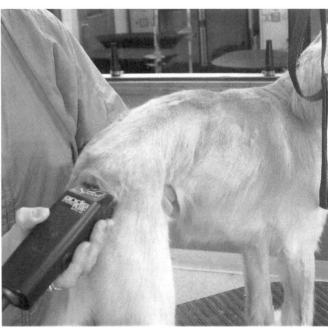

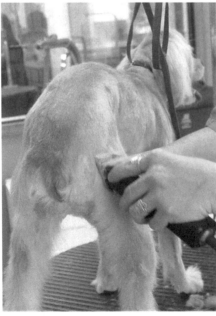

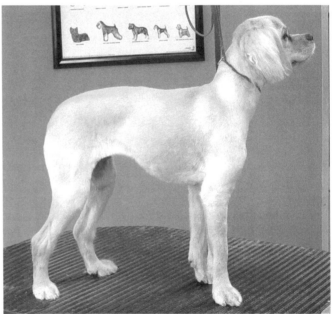

TIPS FOR GETTING IT SMOOTH WITH SPEED AND EASE

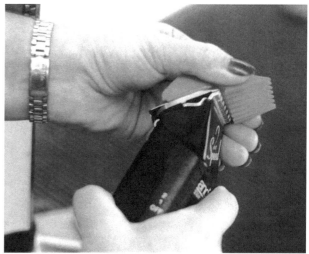

- Stretch the skin on really dense coats to expand the hair follicles per square inch and allow the clipper to cut more easily.

- Move the clipper as quickly as possible, but avoid producing "corduroy markings," which are rough markings in the coat that can be caused by too much hair being fed into the blades at one time.

- Attach-on guard combs will cut when fitted over a number of blades ranging from a #50 to a #10.

- The #40 blade will give the smoothest cut when used under most plastic style guard combs.

- A #30 or longer blade ***must*** be used under the metal styled guard combs. Why? They will break the finer teeth of the #40 or #50 blades rendering them useless once the clipper is running.

Grooves

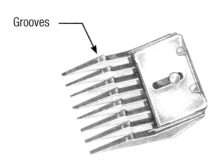

- When an attach-on guard comb fails to glide smoothly through the coat, check to see whether it is clean between the blade and the guard comb. Excessive hair build-up can clog the cutting action. If there is a build up of hair between the blade and the comb, simply remove the build up and resume trimming.

- If you are working with a plastic style guard comb, and hair build-up is not the problem, check for small groove lines just above where it hooks on to the blade teeth. These small grooves can cause the guard comb to "drag" through the coat. Replace with a new guard comb if this is a problem.

TIPS FOR GETTING IT SMOOTH WITH SPEED AND EASE

You will need to go over most pets three times before the coat is really smooth. With most blades, the strokes are long and smooth.

1 The first time removes bulk.

2 The second time removes any high spots.

3 The third time addresses any areas previously missed.

4 Finished dog after going over the pet three times.

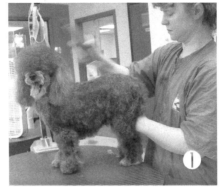
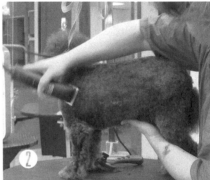

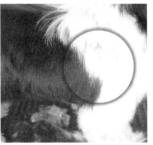

When using an attach-on guard comb on a thick coated dog, the stroke is short and repeated three times in one small section before moving on. As soon as you feel a slight resistance in the cutting action, slightly back the guard comb out and start the stroke again. Normally, on the third pass, the blade cuts cleanly through and you have a nice smooth section left. Repeat the process letting momentum and rhythm work in your favor.

TIPS FOR GETTING IT SMOOTH WITH SPEED AND EASE

• Legs require more attention because their surface is not as flat, say, as on the body. Try running a blade down your own finger to get the idea. So, when clipping legs, the actual contact of the cutting blade is minimal. Also, legs will require a few more passes to get the same results as three passes on flatter areas.

• **Back brush — back brush — back brush**

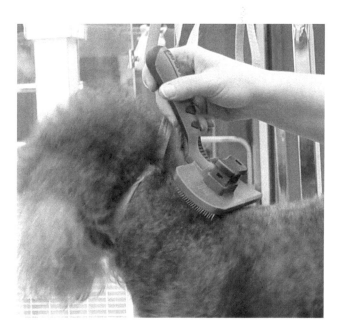

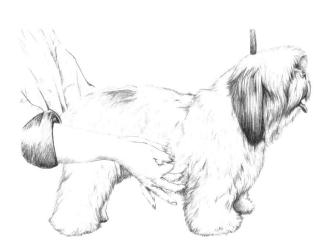

• On drop coated pets trimmed with a longer attach-on guard comb, it's ideal to have the coat set up as though the pet had just shaken its body.

• If the pet won't shake, use a body roll technique to set the coat up as this simulates a natural shake. Stand behind the dog and grasp small tufts of fur between your fingers at the 4 and 8 o'clock positions on the dog's sides. Gently and quickly tug from side to side two or three times to mimic a dog's natural shake.

TIPS ON MAKING THE PET LOOK NEAT

- There should be no stray hairs anywhere.

- If the face is trimmed, is the eye area even? What about the stop area between the eyes?

- Make sure the coat is a consistent length over all the clipped areas.

- In many cases, the tail needs some minor work to make it look neat and balanced with the rest of the dog.

- Clean. Clean. Clean.

Make sure the ears are shaped the same and are equal in length.

Feet, armpits, around the base of the ears, under the tail and the tummy are key areas to look for stray hairs. Double-check these areas.

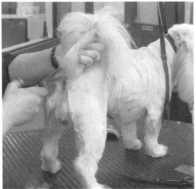
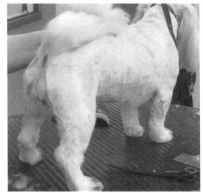

TIPS ON MAKING THE PET LOOK NEAT

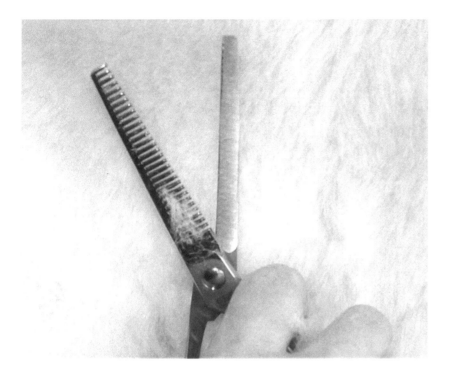

For safety with final detailing, use thinning shears to take off high spots or to buffer a rough spot when working close to the skin.

Clipper Danger Areas: Tuck-up at the flank, the flap of skin under the front leg; where the ear connects to the skull; and the top of the hock on toy-sized dogs. Make sure you are not running your blade parallel to these areas so the skin does not feed into the teeth of the blade.

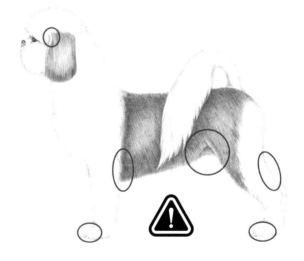

Key Danger Areas On Closely-Trimmed Dogs

Bladed Body / Stylized Leg

A WAY TO SHOW YOUR STUFF

With minor variations, this trim pattern can be adapted to a wide range of purebred and mixed breed dogs. It's stylish and easy to maintain with moderate care between haircuts. The style lends itself nicely to breed profile trimming and corrective grooming techniques. A knowledgeable groomer/stylist in breed profiles and technical techniques can really demonstrate some flair with this trim, if they choose.

PET DOG BREEDS COMMONLY SUITED TO THIS TRIM STYLE:

Sporting Group

Irish Water Spaniel

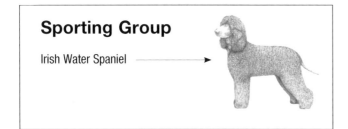

Working Group

Giant Schnauzer
Portuguese Water Dog
Standard Schnauzer

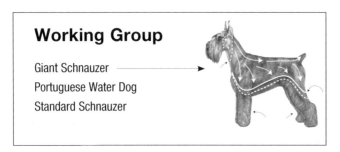

Terrier Group

Airedale Terrier
Bedlington Terrier
Dandie Dinmont Terrier
Wire Fox Terrier
Irish Terrier
Kerry Blue Terrier
Lakeland Terrier
Miniature Schnauzer
Soft Coated Wheaten Terrier
Welsh Terrier

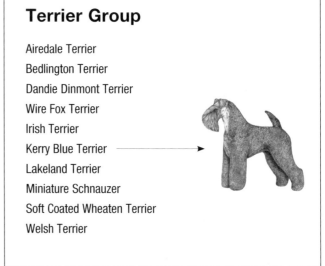

Toy Group

Havanese
Maltese
Poodle
Shih Tzu
Yorkshire Terrier

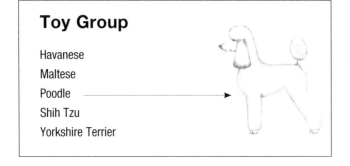

Non-Sporting Group

Bichon Frise
Lhasa Apso
Löwchen
Poodle
Tibetan Terrier

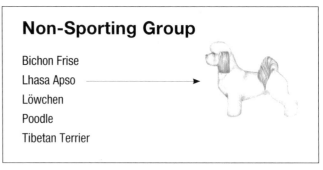

Herding Group

Bearded Collie
Bouvier des Flandres
Briard
Old English Sheepdog
Puli

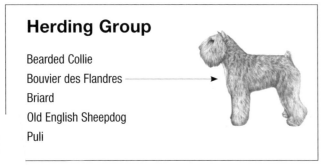

Miscellaneous Group

Pumi

37

Note: Doodles and other many other mixed are well suited to this trim style.

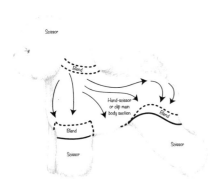

Bichon Frise

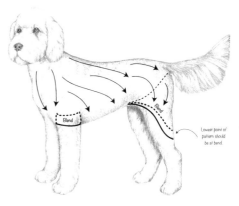

Doodle

Kerry Blue

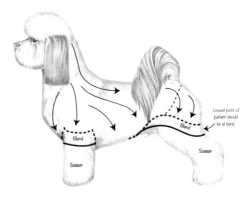

Lhasa Apso

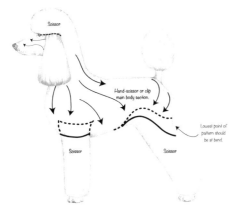

Poodle

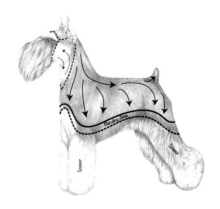

Miniature Schnauzer

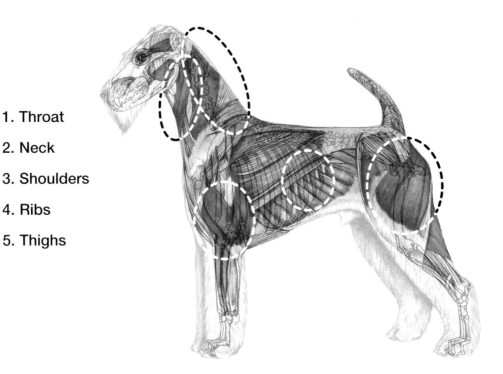

The basic pattern is set by the muscle and bone structure of the dog. Clipper work can vary in length from something as short as a #10 blade to super-long attach-on combs. Some breeds will have a bit of a crest at the back of the neck where longer fur is commonly left. Other breeds will have a small amount of coat left on their undercarriage or at the brisket to accentuate the depth of chest.

5 AREAS MAKE UP THE KEY POINTS FOR SETTING PATTERNS

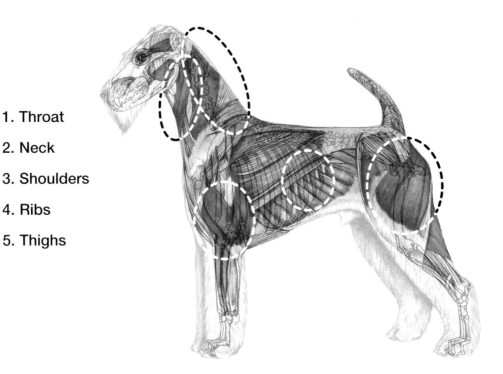

1. Throat

2. Neck

3. Shoulders

4. Ribs

5. Thighs

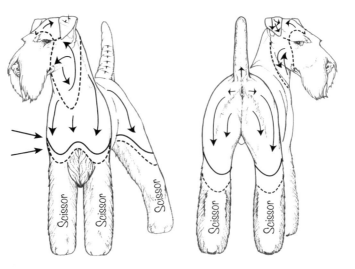

- The pattern lines for the front legs start just where the shoulder muscle starts to turn under.

- This is the top of the blending section and ends right at the elbow.

- For the hip, the top portion of the thigh is trimmed to show off a powerful rear.

- You can feel the upper thigh muscle as you run your hand over this region. The coat on the buttocks is shorter than the legs, similar in length to the body.

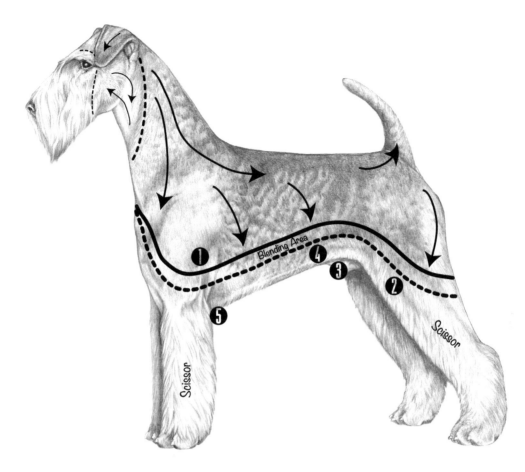

With the undercarriage, some breeds have their entire rib cage area clipped while others have a slight fringe. This fringe will accentuate the depth of chest.

❶ If fringe is left the blending line will start just behind the shoulder and run on a diagonal up and over the flank. (Opposed to a breed where the undercarriage coat is totally removed. E.g. Poodle or Bichon.)

❷ For the rear legs, the pattern line will run on a diagonal from the tuck-up area, over the top of the stifle and toward an area just above the hock. The highest point to this diagonal blending line will start at the flank, with a line running across to the bend of the knee on the back of the rear leg.

❸ The fur should be long enough in the flank area to control the placement of the tuck-up, the bend of the stifle and the angulation of the rear leg just above the hock.

❹ If there is fringe left, the shortest section on the underside of the dog, will be placed close to the last two ribs.

❺ To create depth of chest, slightly longer fur can be left in the brisket area.

When viewed from a few feet away, all pattern and blending lines should be invisible from blending and feathering the shorter coat into the longer hair.

WHAT ARE YOUR GOALS FOR THIS GROOMING JOB?

The goals of this trim are to present a cute or stylish trim on a pet, accentuating the proper breed profile whenever possible. Balance, style and symmetry coupled with excellent technical skills all play a role in a pleasing outcome.

TIPS FOR ACHIEVING SMOOTH SCISSOR WORK

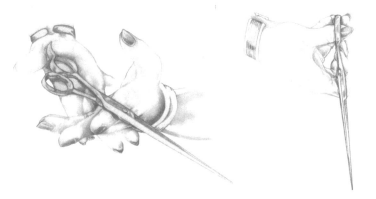

- Use a variety of attach-on guard combs to carve, shape and mold the coat.

- Correctly manipulate your clippers over the body of the pet to minimize how much scissor work you need to do. This is key at the transition areas between clipper and scissored areas.

- Hold the shears correctly: thumb and ring finger, stretch out to the "balance point" of the shear. Open and close the shear with only your thumb. Keep the shear at right angles to your hand.

- Scissor with your body. Do not bounce straight or curved shears on the coat as you trim. Bouncing normally stems from someone who is standing still, scissoring from their shoulder. When this happens, the hand has a strong tendency to bounce as the groomer runs the scissors along the coat.

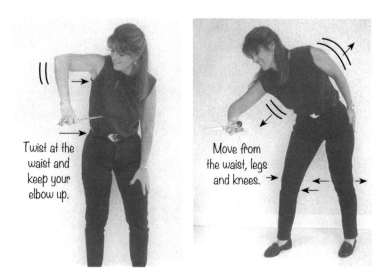

Twist at the waist and keep your elbow up.

Move from the waist, legs and knees.

Think of scissoring as though the shears were a laser beam. If you bounce the beam, the scissor finish will be rough. Stay steady and you'll get that smooth, velvet finish we are all looking for.

TIPS ON KEEPING THE TRIM LOOKING NATURAL

- On many of the sporting dogs, less is more—don't clipper the back coat unless requested to by a client or the coat is very unruly. Instead, use simple carding and hand-stripping techniques.

- When clipping, choose a longer blade length—such as a #7F, #5F, #4F or even longer—to easily blend the shorter areas into the longer, natural ones.

- Transition lines need a fair amount of room to make the pattern lines invisible due to the nature of the coat and techniques used to blend the two areas.

- "Carding" removes soft undercoat. It can be done by pulling a number of tools through the coat, working with the grain; A #40 blade held between your fingers, a fine-toothed stripping knife, or a lava-like pumice stone.

- Blend heavily, using a combination of top thinning and bulk thinning methods. You should not be able to see a pattern line when you are a few feet from the pet.

- Normally, the lower outline of the pet is left more natural with only minor shaping of the furnishings, unless the owner requests length taken off for ease of coat care.

Invest in the best thinning shears you can afford. Good ones are worth their weight in gold.

BLENDERS AND THINNING SHEAR DEFINITIONS

Top Thinning: Top thinning is when the coat is trimmed from the top, removing length, leaving a very soft and natural look. The hand will bounce slightly with each cut, clearing the cut fur out of the way for the next cut, allowing the stylist to see the progress.

Bulk Thinning: Bulk thinning is done to remove bulk from an area in the coat while maintaining a very natural look with longer fur. To bulk thin an area, open the blades of your thinning shears. Insert the shear under the fur. Focus on the bulky area that needs to be smoothed down. The smooth blade will glide along the dog's body while the toothed blade is beveled away from the skin, eliminating the risk of cutting or pinching the dog's skin. Make one cut then extract the shear, brushing the cut coat out with a heavy slicker brush. If the area needs more work, repeat the cut, brush process until you have achieved the look you desire. The key to success with bulk thinning is to work slowly, constantly removing the trimmed fur to as you go to monitor your progress.

Hand-Scissored & Miscellaneous Trims

THE ARTIST IN YOU CAN SHINE

Hand-scissored trim is where artists and sculptors step up to the grooming table. A gifted stylist can mold and shape fur into unbelievable shapes. They bring out the best points of the pet and hide the flaws. When finished, the coat looks like velvet, without a mark, divot or line in the flawless finish. High quality hand-scissoring is nearly a lost art, but when it's executed correctly, combined with an exceptional knowledge of breed profile trimming, the final trim can be simply breathtaking.

Miscellaneous Styles are in the minority for most professional grooming salons doing everyday trims. The dogs that are normally put into these trims are few and far between. Some groomers enjoy the challenge these trims pose such as lion trims or owner created trims.

PET DOG BREEDS COMMONLY SUITED TO LONGER OR UNIQUE HAND-SCISSORED TRIM STYLES:

Chow Chow

Poodle

Portuguese Water Dog
(Curly Coated)

Shih Tzu

Although these breeds might have owners requesting unique or longer hand-scissored trim styles, those requests are typically uncommon in a salon's day-to-day business.

Sporting Group

Irish Water Spaniel

Hound Group

Afghan Hound

Working Group

Portuguese Water Dog

Samoyed

Terrier Group

Kerry Blue Terrier

Skye Terrier

Soft Coated Wheaten Terrier

Toy Group

Chinese Crested (Powderpuff)

Havanese

Maltese

Poodle

Shih Tzu

Pomeranian

Yorkshire Terrier

Non-Sporting Group

American Eskimo Dog

Bichon Frise

Chow Chow

Keeshond

Lhasa Apso

Löwchen

Poodle

Tibetan Terrier

Herding Group

Bearded Collie

Bouvier des Flandres

Briard

Collie

Old English Sheepdog

Puli

Shetland Sheepdog

Herding Group

Bearded Collie

Bouvier des Flandres

Briard

Collie

Old English Sheepdog

Puli

Shetland Sheepdog

54

HAND-SCISSOR TRIM

It's easier to master this art of hand-scissoring on some coats—such as thick and tightly curled—than on others. When you push your hand down on such a coat, its density causes it to spring right back into place. The most difficult coat to work with is considered the drop coat, such as is found on Shih Tzus and Malteses. These coats lack curl and body. If a stylist is not highly proficient with his scissoring skills, every cut with shears will show on such a coat, producing a flawed trim. Having excellent shears and knowing how to use them is the key to perfecting this trim. For curly coated dogs, you'll need straight and curved shears. For dogs with coats that lack fullness and body, you'll want to add a high quality thinning shear to the collection. Excellent eye-to-hand coordination is necessary to produce this haircut.

It takes years of practice and study to master this art. The hand-scissored trim is rare in those professional pet styling salons where most pet owners seek low maintenance trims. *(Intergroom: Best in Show line-up)*

This high level of art is usually seen in contest styling arenas, in the conformation rings and high end salons. Such trims are the true test of a highly skilled professional pet stylist.

One of the best ways to learn the secrets of fine hand-scissoring is to sit ringside and watch these masters at work.

WHAT ARE YOUR GOALS FOR THIS HAND-SCISSORED GROOMING JOB?

The goal for this trim style is to correctly interpret the breed profile of the dog, creating a trim that is stylish and well balanced with flawlessly executed technical skills.

TIPS FOR HAND-SCISSORING

- Hold the shears correctly using your thumb and ring finger. Open and close the shear with your thumb while the rest of your hand remains steady.

- Stretch your hand out to the balance point on the shear shank to stabilize it.

- With smooth-bladed shears, don't bounce the shear off the coat.

- With thinning shears, bounce slightly to clear the hair before cutting again.

- A clean, well-prepared coat is critical—no mats, tangles, or loose coat.

- A perfectly hand blown dry or fluff dry coat is the only way to get a velvet finish.

- Study the breed standard for different breeds and be able to interpret the standard into correct grooming language.

- Study anatomy, structure, movement and canine psychology to get a clear grasp of your subject matter.

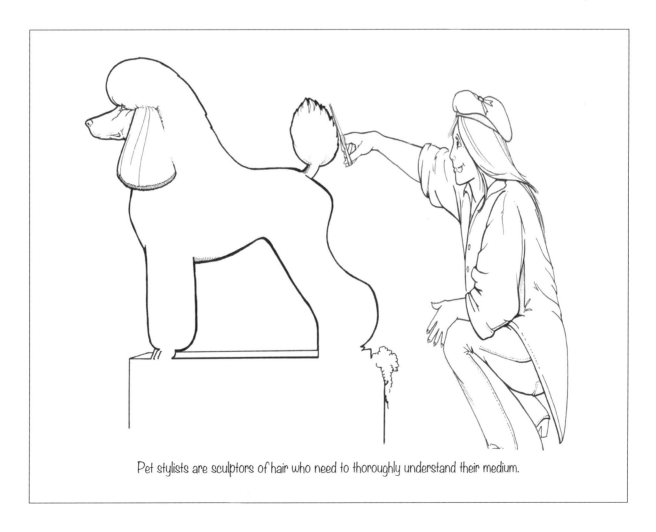

Pet stylists are sculptors of hair who need to thoroughly understand their medium.

MISCELLANEOUS TRIM: LION TRIM

There are a couple breeds where this trim style is the 'correct' trim for the breed. We see it with the Portuguese Water Dog and the Löwchen. For some owners, a lion trim is a great option on their pet dogs. It offers style and flair to some pets while minimizing the maintenance of the fur. Typical breeds seen with this trim option are the; Pomeranian, Chow Chow and Golden Retriever. However, this trim is suitable for any breed of dog that carries a coat as well as long coated cats.

❶ There a couple options to setting the pattern. One option is to set the pattern at the withers. Another option is to place the pattern line near the last rib. Use the breed standard or the owners preference to set the pattern line.

❷ The close work can be done with blades ranging from a #15 to a #4F or even shorter guard combs use with or against the grain based on the breed, coat type, climate and client preference. In cooler climates, the closely trimmed sections may be clipped longer for the comfort of the dog. The entire rear area of the pet is clipped close while the head, neck, shoulder, chest and sometimes the rib areas are left full.

❸ Trimming the front legs is optional on some pets but if it is done, use the same blade as used on the rear section. Clear the entire front leg from the elbow to the foot.

❹ There is a tuft left at the end of the tail in the shape of a plume. The plume can include the last half to last third of the tail bone.

❺ The longer areas can be left natural or trimmed to accentuate the shape.

TIPS FOR THE LION TRIM

- Use reference points on the body to set the pattern such as the ribs or withers.

- Confirm with the owners if they want the neck left natural or sculpted.

- Using a blade in reverse will enhance the speed and quality of the close clipper work.

Ask the owner if they want a 'young' or a 'mature' lion trim. A younger lion will carry less mane while the mature lion will have a full, thick ruff.

① ② ③ ④ ❺

OWNER CREATED TRIMS

These are the hardest to control the overall quality and balance of the trim. Most owners don't have an eye for breed profile trimming or stylish balance. They create trims that are easier for them to care for while retaining some attributes they really like, such as the long hair on a Lhasa. A common thread that runs through many of these "owner created" trims have shaved feet and legs. Some salons or professionals won't even consider doing these requests due to the lack of appeal the trim has, no matter how well executed.

TIPS FOR OWNER CREATED TRIMS

• Listen to the owner. Confirm your interpretation of what you hear for clarity.

• Photos are worth 1000 words. Encourage the client to bring in a photo of the trim they have in mind for their pet.

HOW MANY BASIC HEAD STYLES ARE THERE?

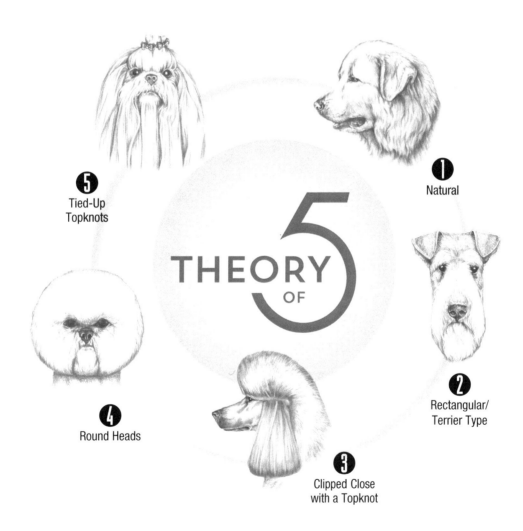

5 Tied-Up Topknots

1 Natural

2 Rectangular/ Terrier Type

3 Clipped Close with a Topknot

4 Round Heads

THEORY OF 5

Natural Head Style

CAN HAPPEN NATURALLY OR MUST BE CREATED

⑤

Typical Dogs with Naturally-Smooth Faces

Golden Retriever

Shetland Sheepdog

Maremma Sheepdog ———————————————————▶

Typical Dogs that Need Help Creating the Natural Face

Cocker Spaniel ———————————————————▶

English Setter

Springer Spaniel

One of the biggest challenges to creating a smooth, natural head is a lot of fur on the cheeks and muzzle of the dog. Such a coat can easily "track," leaving atrocious clipper marks. Clipping both with and against the grain of the coat growth is one way to overcome this challenge. Use blades ranging from a #15 all the way up to a #4F blade.

The goal of this head style is a natural look, a simple task when it grows that way. When faced with an overabundance of coat on the head and muzzle regions, simulating the natural short coat growth with clippers and other tools is the target.

Pet dogs that already have nice, neat muzzles are easy—leave it alone.

Don't cut off the whiskers unless the client requests they be removed, which is rare with a pet dog.

TIPS FOR REMOVING EXCESSIVE FACIAL COAT

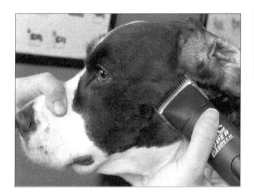  

- Don't clip areas that are naturally tight and short. Instead, feather and blend longer coat into shorter areas on the muzzle with clippers and thinning shears.

- Use "F" blades in reverse to get a smooth, clean cut. In most cases, a blade used against the lay of the coat will trim two blade lengths shorter than when used with the lay of the coat.

- If the coat is extremely thick, stretch the skin and slow the clipper stroke to minimize the amount of coat being fed into the clipper teeth at one time. Feeding too much coat into the clipper blade causes unsightly corduroy tracking.

- If tracking cannot be totally eliminated, use thinning shears and a pumice stone to help minimize the marks.

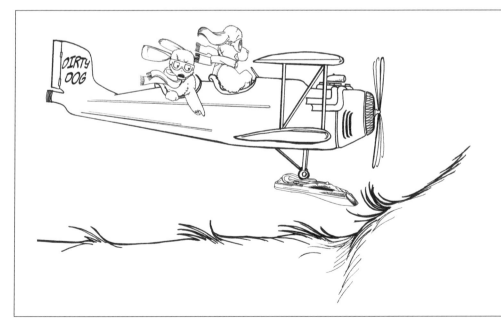

When clipping into transitional areas, think of a plane coming in for a "touch-and-go" landing: gently glide in, touch down and smoothly take off again without stopping.

Rectangular Head Style

THE LINES OF THE FACE FORM THE SHAPE

The rectangular head style is normally found on terrier breeds and some working dogs. There are minor differences between breeds in the length and density of the rectangle stemming from the bone structure of the dog. Beard length is another controlling factor. Eye areas, too, can vary from small triangular split brows to long exaggerated ones to no split at all, creating a fall instead. The common denominator between these heads is the overall shape—a series of straight lines that form a rectangle. The primary lines are at the top of the head and the sides of the face. Leaving fill under the eyes is a vital element in creating this straight line look at the sides of the face.

TYPICAL BREEDS WITH RECTANGLE HEAD STYLES:

Rectangular Heads with Short Triangular Brows & Tapered Beards

Airedale

Wire Fox Terrier

Irish Terrier

Welsh Terrier

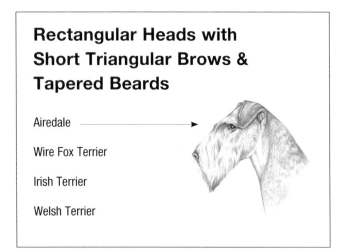

Rectangular Heads with Long Exaggerated Brows & Beards

Giant Schnauzer

Miniature Schnauzer

Scottish Terrier

Standard Schnauzer

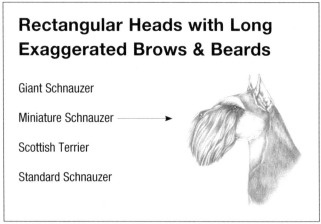

Rectangular Heads with Falls

Kerry Blue Terrier

Lakeland Terrier

Sealyham Terrier

Soft Coated Wheaten Terrier

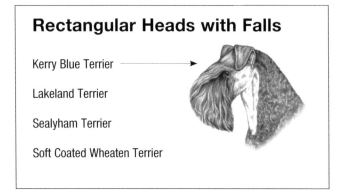

A few other wire-coated breeds from other groups loosely follow the rectangular head style as well with small brows or falls.

For most of these breeds, the top skull is closely trimmed to show off the level line of the head between the ears. Dogs with exaggerated brows are trimmed closest, about the length of a #10 blade used with the grain. Small triangular brows traditionally have a bit more coat on the top of the head—the amount produced by roughly a #7F blade used with the lay of the coat. On dogs with falls, clipper length varies from close trimming on the top of the head as on the Kerry Blue, or to the Wheaten, which has the longest coat left on the top of the head, up to a full inch.

The general lines for clipping the neck, throat and cheek vary slightly, but all clear the throat area enough to show off a moderate length of neck that is powerful. Typical blades used to clip the neck, throat and cheek range from a #15 to a medium sized attach-on comb for the Wheaten. Dogs with exaggerated brows usually are clipped shortest, while short-browed dogs are a bit longer. Again, the dogs with falls vary. The Kerry is done very close, the Sealyham is a bit longer and the Wheaten goes the longest. The line for the cheek starts just behind the eye and follows the bony ridge straight back to the ear canal. The line establishing the beard starts just behind the back corner of the eye and runs on a diagonal toward the back corner of the mouth. On some breeds, the line will stop before the mouth, on others it goes right to the mouth. Certain breeds have heavier goatees than others, but the general rule of thumb with all of them (other than the Schnauzers and the Soft Coated Wheaten) is that the line under the chin that forms the goatee is brought slightly farther forward than the back corner of the mouth. With the Schnauzers, the basic lines of the beard and goatee are set by the three whisker nodulars found on the muzzle, 2 on either side of the cheeks and one under the jaw. The throat and neck line starts at the base of the ear, or ear bulb. It drops to a soft "V" with the bottom of the "V" resting a few inches above the breast bone; the larger the dog, the greater the distance.

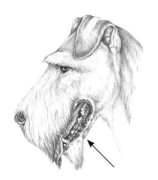

The coat on the muzzle making up the beard and goatee vary in length from breed to breed. The coat under the eye area is never clipped as this hair forms one of the critical lines of the classic rectangular head style. The line on the dog's face should be straight, from the flat cheek down into the beard area. Double-check this line by laying a greyhound comb along the side of the head. Any fur that sticks out beyond the comb should be removed. Any hair inside this line needs to remain and is to be blended to create the rectangular shape.

Groomed   Not Groomed

On dogs with long, natural beards, the lines making up the head are sharp, crisp and clean. On the shorter beards and brows of the harsh coated terriers, the lines are blended to be invisible. Check this line by holding the beard and goatee coat in your hand, holding it out of the way. Look for stray or long hairs at the junction of the clipped areas on the checks and throat and the beard/goatee. Make sure the line is neat.

TIPS TO HELP SET A RECTANGULAR HEAD

❶
• Use the eye socket ridge to set the brow. This will help in getting them even.

• On dogs with short brows and harsh coats, clip the top skull with the lay of the hair for better blending.

• For dogs with long beards and exaggerated brows (except on the Wheaten), use a #7F–#5F or #4F blade in reverse to set the lines over the brows or fall.

❷
• On long brows, to help facilitate matching brows, use reference points. With shears pointing towards the nose and beveled away from the skin, place the shear near the back corner of the eye. Line the tips of the shears at a particular area on the nose. On the opposite brow, use the same reference points when trimming to get the same size and shape of the first brow.

• Use curved shears in reverse to set long brows and falls.

❸
• Trim small brows with thinning shears to eliminate a sharp line, allowing the brow to accentuate the piercing expression of the dog, but blending with the overall look of the haircut where all lines are blended and invisible.

❹
• On dogs that have shorter beards and brows, shorten the longer hair in the muzzle area by raking a medium-length guard comb over the beard area. Feather off over the end of the muzzle to extend the length of the rectangular head.

• With long exaggerated brows, remove the cowlicks that are found just at the inside corner of the eye, otherwise the brows will cross over one another.

• On long-bearded dogs, hold the entire beard in your hand and check the line between the long coat and the clipped throat and cheek areas.

• With short-bearded dogs, blend the transition line between the cheeks and the beard with thinning shears to help create an invisible line.

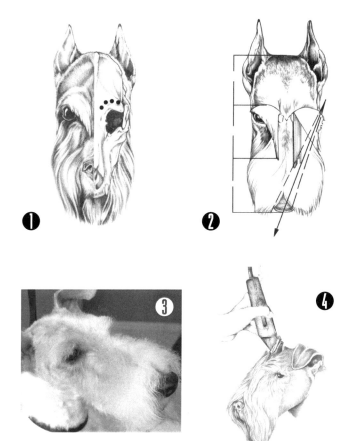

When drying long brows, add a small amount of styling gel or hair spray while the coat is still wet. Comb or brush the product into the fur. Set the brows with warm air from the dryer.

Clipped Close with a Topknot

ADAPTABLE TO MANY BREEDS

When we think of this head style, most of us think of the Poodle, however, there are other breeds that have a variation of this head style and it adapts to many mixed breed styles, too. When a muzzle area is clipped close, it should always be exceptionally neat and tidy, free of any uneven or rough areas. The lines are crisp and clean.

TYPICAL DOGS WITH CLEAN FACES AND TOPKNOTS

Poodle

Irish Water Spaniel

Chinese Crested

Poodle and Poodle-Mix Topknots

The goal of this head style is to accentuate the regal, elegant and intelligent look of a Poodle and Poodle-type mixes. Whatever the shape—flared, straight-sided or rounded—the topknot should always be a well balanced extension of the skull. It should be impeccably neat and symmetrical.

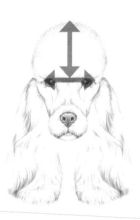

The topknot on a Poodle or a Poodle-mix should be an extension of the skull. The cheekbones will help distinguish your guidelines for the size and shape of the topknot. The height of the topknot should be roughly as high as the distance between the back corners of the eyes.

The topknot is set using landmark points on the skull as reference. The clipped line on the sides of the face that helps to establish the topknot runs from the ear canal opening to the back corner of the eye. It will parallel the zygomatic arch, which is easily felt.

The coat over the eyes should be steeply beveled, creating a deep-set eye and an intelligent expression.

Chinese Crested and Irish Water Spaniel Topknots

On the Chinese Crested and Irish Water Spaniel the topknot is left more natural in shape while the clipped lines are clean and crisp.

For efficient clipping, it's important to gently stretch the skin back toward the ear, but not up into the topknot area. Stretching the skin upward will destroy the natural, straight line from the ear canal to the back of the eye. Continue clipping forward, under the eye and down the bridge of the nose.

To easily clip the lip area, place a finger at the back corner of the mouth and stretch the skin. Be careful not to catch the smooth skin ridges just on the inside of the lips on the lower jaw.

For safety, ride that area with only the edge of the clipper blade, minimizing the chance of the ridges slipping between the cutting teeth. Hold the clipper softly, in a supple hand, as it glides over the skin.

At the stop area, clip an inverted "V" to give definition to the eyes and to lengthen the muzzle. If you are clipping the face cleanly, work over the muzzle area and the lower jaw. If you are leaving a mustache, clip a diagonal line halfway down the nose, leaving fur on the end of the muzzle.

For the lower jaw, come forward just a bit to create a goatee. By clearing the very back mouth corner of hair, you will get a neat appearance when the pet opens its mouth to pant.

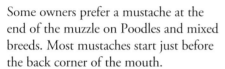

Some owners prefer a mustache at the end of the muzzle on Poodles and mixed breeds. Most mustaches start just before the back corner of the mouth.

For the upper jaw, or nose, follow a line from the back of the mouth forward to about halfway to the nose on a diagonal.

Mustaches can easily be created by using a longer blade or guard comb to set the length. Once the length is set, only minor neatening is required by hand.

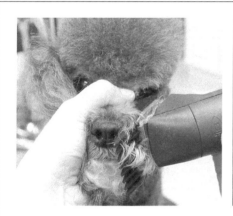

An easy way to create a pet mustache is with a clipper. Based on the size of the pet and fullness of the mustache, blade choices range from a #4F to a long guard comb. Work with the grain to remove the bulk of the coat. Then follow up with some light hand shaping with scissors or thinning shears. When trimming around the muzzle area, make sure to hold the mouth firmly closed—keeping the tongue in the mouth and avoiding accidentally nicking it.

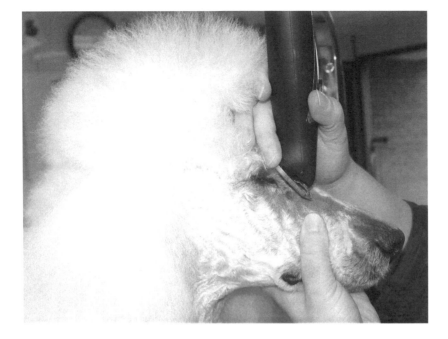

TIPS FOR CREATING A CLIPPED FACE WITH A STYLIZED TOPKNOT

- For most pets, a #10 used in reverse with a soft hand and a relaxed wrist is safe and will not cause clipper irritation. Occasionally, on dark skinned pets, a closer blade can be used without harming the skin. On light colored pets or very thinly coated pets, a longer blade is a better choice to minimize the risk of clipper sensitivity.

- In most cases, going against the grain will give you the cleanest results and the most immaculate lines. On pets that are prone to clipper irritation, a longer blade or a blade used with the direction of the coat growth may be a better option, even though quality is usually compromised.

- To discern the line that separates the topknot from the face, feel for the bony ridge that runs parallel from the back corner of the eye to the ear canal opening. This is the line you will use for your clipper work. Use care when clipping as to not stretch the skin which can give you a false vision of where this lies.

Clipping higher than the correct line can give you a strange look.

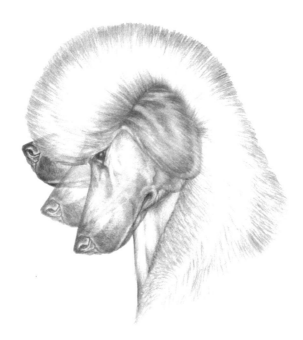

The pattern for the neck and throat is shaped in a "V" or a "U." It accentuates an elegant neck. The "V" or "U" will start at the ear bulbs and plunge downward, stopping at the Adams Apple or just before the throat starts to indent towards the chest. Some stylists use the end of the nose as a general reference point for setting the depth of the "V" or "U"-shaped neckline. While the dog is standing squarely, ask the dog to tip its nose toward the chest. Where the end of the nose falls is the lowest point of the neckline. If the dog has a very short muzzle, the line may be drawn slightly farther down.

The neck line should be deep enough to accentuate a strong, elegant neck.

HOW TO CUT A TOPKNOT

There are many methods for trimming topknots, but here is an easy one for the floppy type we commonly see in our salons. We call it the side, side-front, back method. Once the face has been clipped, the topknot can be shaped for Poodle-styled topknots.

❶ Comb all the hair over to one side.

Flip the ear over the top of the head to minimize the risk of nicking the ear leather where it joins the skull.

Glide a pair of opened, straight shears under the clipped line that separates the cheek from the topknot.

Rest the lower blade of the shear softly on the skin. Always bevel the shear slightly away from the skin to avoid cutting or catching the skin between the blades when they close.

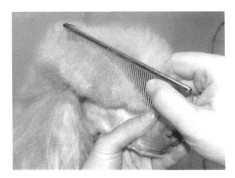

❷ Flip the ear over and glide the shear over the top of it, right at the junction point of the skull and the leather.

When gliding shears over the tops of the ears, always lift the tips of the shears before you cut to ensure you have only fur between your shear blades and not a section of the ear leather.

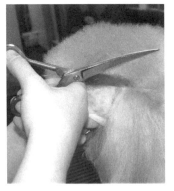

❸ Working back-to-front, hold the ear gently taut and bevel the shear slightly before cutting the line around the ear, wrapping right around the base of the ear, connecting the line of the topknot into the clipper line of the throat.

Repeat the process on the opposite side of the head.

4   Next, comb all the hair forward over the eyes.

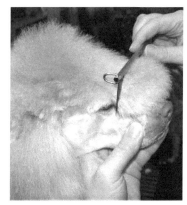

5   Glide the opened shear in at a steep bevel. The fur just above the eyes will be very short, but longer as it gently angles away. Once set, this stacked ledge holds hair away from the eyes and gives them a deep-set appearance, creating an intelligent expression for the pet.

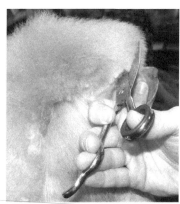 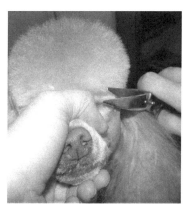

6   Join the topknot line with the neckline so it is one, flowing line. Comb all the hair to the back and blend the fur into the neck.

With curved shears, round the top edge and check that all lines are well blended, neat and clean.

When trimming behind the topknot, hold the dog's head in an upright natural position so the top edge of the topknot is not removed in the trimming process.

7   Give the ears a small tug-tug, alternating between ears to simulate a mild, natural head shake.

Fluff the topknot with a comb.

Check the work from all angles, front, side and rear.

The Round Head

SHAPING THE FUR

Round heads can be created on many different purebreds and mixed breed dogs—if the dog grows longer fur on its face, a round head style can be shaped. The overall look will vary from dog to dog based on skull type, ear set, muzzle length and coat type.

THERE ARE THREE BASIC COAT TYPES THAT APPLY TO ROUND HEAD STYLING ON ALL DOGS, PUREBRED, OR MIXED BREED:

Drop Coats
(such as the Shih Tzu)

Curly & Wavy Coats
(such as the Bichon Frise)

Wire Coats
(such as the West Highland White Terrier)

The process to create the head style will differ with each coat type, however, the common goal remains the same —to focus the eyes and nose at the center of the headpiece for a balanced finished product.

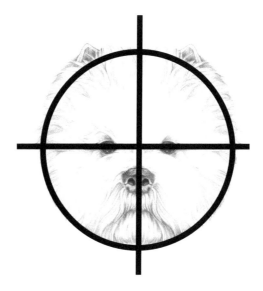

DROP COATED HEAD STYLING

There are a number of different ways to create a round head style on a dog, but the two simplest are done with a clipper. The length will vary based on client preference and length of body coat. It's most important the head be in balance with the body. With both styles outlined here, the stop area should be trimmed very close, either with thinning shears or by clipping with a close blade, such as a #10 or a #15. This will clear the eyes of long fur and accentuate a nice, deep-set eye.

STYLE OPTION #1

A short low maintenance head style following the natural growth coat pattern of the head.

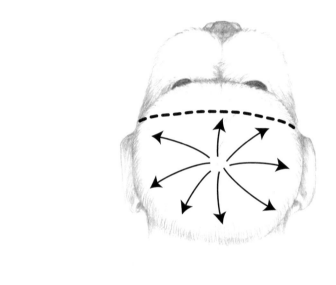

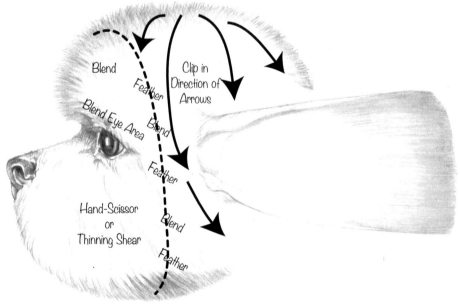

STYLE OPTION #1

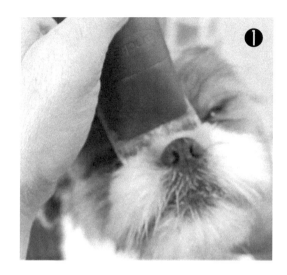

❶ Pre-clip the stop area between the eyes with a #10 or #15 blade with a light touch *or* use thinning shears to clear longer fur from the stop area.

❷ There will be an imaginary line just behind the eyes where you can feel the eye socket rims. This will be your pattern line for your clipper work.

Then, take the same blade used to trim the body and use it again for the top of the head and down the sides of the face. If a #4F, #5F, #7F or shorter guard comb was used on the body, follow the natural lay of the coat, working out from the center of the skull.

❸ Once clipper work is complete, use thinning shears to blend, soften and neaten the fur.

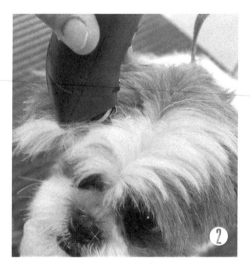

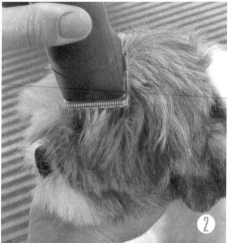

STYLE OPTION #2

This is a longer and fuller round head style using a guard comb.

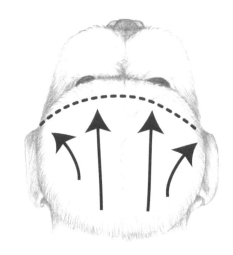

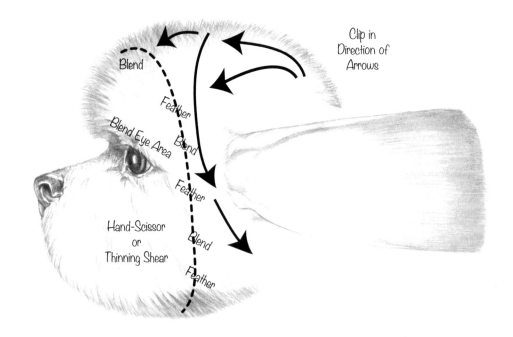

STYLE OPTION #2

Pre-clip the stop area between the eyes with a #10 or #15 blade with a light touch *or* use thinning shears to clear longer fur from the stop area.

❶ There will be an imaginary line just behind the eyes where you can feel the eye socket rims. All fur behind your hands is clipped. All hair in front of this line is left to do by hand with shears.

❷ The second style is to use medium to longer guard combs for small- to medium-sized pets; longer combs can be used on larger dogs. Due to the length of coat these combs leave, they are most effective when pulled forward from the occiput to the framed area of the eye. The hair over the eyes in this area should be left to hand-scissor, framing the eyes in the final stages of the trim.

❸ Lift the ear out of the way and come down the sides of the face, into the jowl area, blending into the clipped neck. Remember to leave just enough hair at the back corners of the eyes to complete the framework for the eyes in the finished trim.

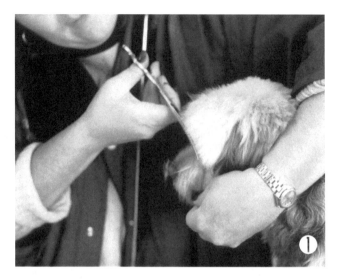

TIPS FOR STYLE OPTIONS #1 AND #2

❶ The framed area over the eyes should be hand-scissored. Comb the hair forward over the eyes, making sure to get the hair in the stop area, too. Scissor off the longer hair at a 45-degree angle, starting at the stop area to create a deep-set eye.

❷ A pair of curved shears in reverse can be helpful to create the framework around the eyes. The coat immediately over each eye is very close and bevels out as it gets farther away. Beveling the fur above the eyes creates a ledge for the longer coat to sit on, keeping it out of the eyes and creating a soft expression. Double-check this line a number of times, as it is the most important part of the entire trim.

❸ Soften the framed area with thinning shears once the correct line is set. Double-check the line just behind the eyes where the clipper work feathers off. It should be smooth and even at the transition point.

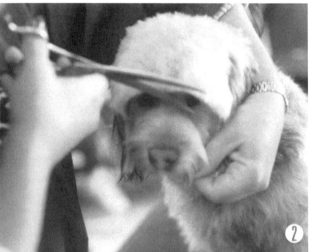

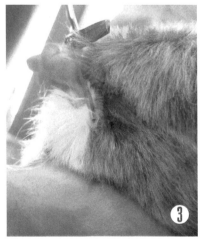

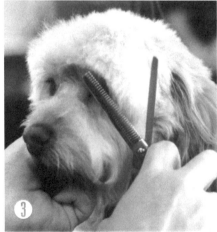

TIPS FOR STYLE OPTIONS #1 AND #2

The muzzle on most round head styles is trimmed by hand, keeping the eyes and nose at the center. There are multiple styling options though and some pet owners prefer the muzzle be left very long. Many stylist find using guard combs on the muzzle area works well in short or medium lengths, but longer styles require hand trimming. The important thing is that the muzzle is evenly shaped and the edges are buffered into a soft, neat line.

 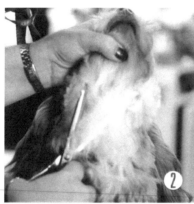

❶ For the muzzle, begin trimming the fur parallel to the jaw bone to the desired length to create a balanced head piece.

❷ Once the fur length on the muzzle has been established, tilt the dogs head back, combing fur down towards the neck. With thinning shears, lightly scissor an inverted "V" at the neck/throat junction. Trimming in this inverted "V" will eliminate a double chin when the head drops into a natural position. With the dog's head in a natural position, comb the underjaw in a downward direction and check for evenness in this entire area.

❸ Gently lift ears away from the neck and double check for neatness in jowl area.

❹ Finish by looking at the dog from all angles looking for a neat, soft round face. If anything is out of place, use thinning shears to correct.

If trimming the muzzle area with a guard comb, make sure to double check your work for smoothness. Comb the coat up and away from the muzzle. Use thinning or blending shears to tidy your work.

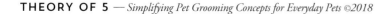

HEAD STYLES: ROUND HEAD

① ② ③ **④** ⑤

TIPS ON CREATING THE ROUND HEAD WITH A CLIPPER

Use the following hold to define sections of the head that are to be clipped or hand-scissored:

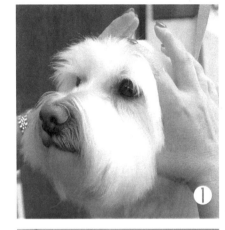

❶ Standing in front of the dog, place your hands just behind the eyes so both thumbs touch under the jaw and both first fingers touch just above the eyes. Anything behind your hands is considered the skull and should be clipped. Anything in front of your fingers is considered the eye area and muzzle and should be shaped by hand (or clipped with a guard comb on the muzzle).

❷ Using a similar hold, place your fingers around the neck of the dog. Slide your hands up until they rest at the base of the ears. This is your dividing line between the neck and headpiece.

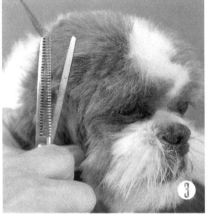

❸ By gently grasping longer ears under the chin, you can easily control the pet and keep the ears separate from the headpiece.

❹ Pulling the ears softly back to the base of the skull allows you to see a clear view of the shape of the head.

These techniques allow for extremely consistent styling from salon to salon and from trim to trim.

FREEHAND-SCISSORED ROUND HEAD STYLE: BICHON TYPE

Curly coated dogs often need the neck coat to be hand-scissored into the head to be balanced with the rest of the trim.

❶ For a Bichon-style head, start with the eye area. Clear the stop area either with clippers or by hand with thinning shears.

❷ Comb the coat forward over the eyes and trim it like the front of a Poodle topknot, at a steep bevel over the eyes.

❸ You can trim just beyond the outer corners of the eyes with the bevel. Recheck your line and detail the beveled line until it is smooth and even.

❹ Next, pull the ears forward to the nose and trim off any ear coat falling beyond the length of the muzzle. This will establish the jaw line for a Bichon-styled head — the ears and jaw are of equal length.

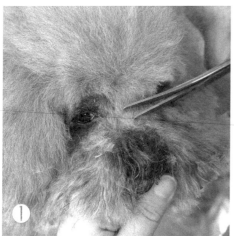

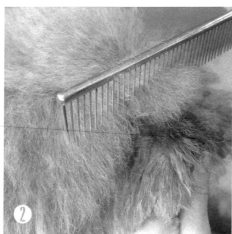

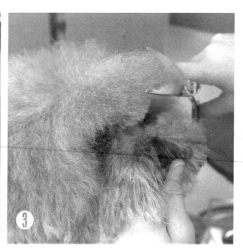

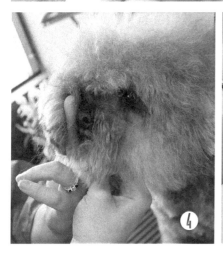

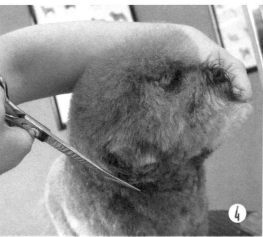

For non-Bichon type round head styles, the ear length can vary from extremely long to super-short clipped ears.

FREEHAND-SCISSORED ROUND HEAD STYLE: BICHON TYPE

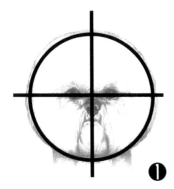

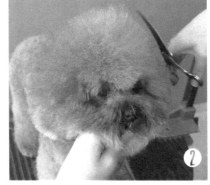

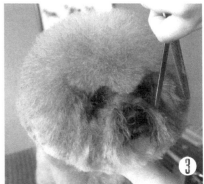

❶ Keep the eyes and nose at the center of the circle.

❷ With a Bichon-type head, there is no break at the ear line, so scissor the topknot and ears into one piece. On mixed breeds, a line can be created over the ear as you would with a Poodle head style.

❸ For the Bichon, the sides of the head are hand-scissored creating the full round head piece. The head can be tapered a bit on the sides for Poodles, Doodles and other mixed breeds by using a long guard comb between the back corner of the eyes and the ear canal. Using a longer guard comb will assist in setting equal lengths from side to side.

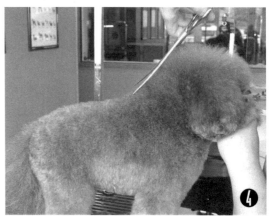

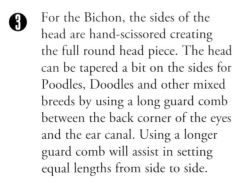

❹ Finish the trim by hand, blending the top of the rounded topknot so that it smoothly flows into the crest of the neck.

❺ The muzzle may be trimmed by hand or, for shorter round heads with this coat type, trimmed with a medium to longer attach-on guard comb. Whether shaped by hand or set with an attach-on comb, double-check the area for neatness with either regular or thinning shears. The finished product should be neat, clean and in pleasing harmony with the rest of the trim.

TIPS FOR CREATING A ROUND HEAD ON CURLY COATED DOGS

- Make sure all curls and kinks are removed in the drying stage.

- The eye area is beveled. Stack the coat above the eyes to keep the hair out of the eyes and create a kind, intelligent expression.

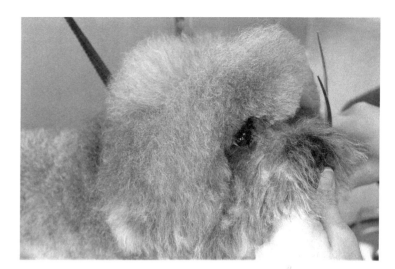

- Double- and triple-check the line above the eyes for evenness.

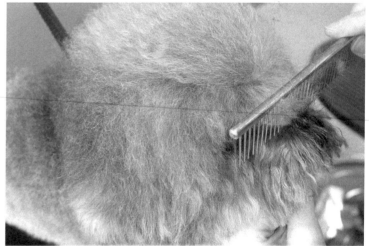

- For large, full head styles, curved shears longer than 8.5 inches are helpful.

- For tighter head styles, set the sides of the face with a guard comb, ensuring evenness from side to side.

- Clasp the ears loosely behind the head to check the overall final head shape as you finish trimming this head style.

HARSH COATED TERRIER TYPE, ROUND HEAD STYLE

When viewed from the front, this head style is full and round. The fur on pet terrier dogs normally does not have the harsh texture required to frame the face the way a hand-stripped coat does, although the same general rules apply. The coat should look very natural, with no scissor marks. The eyes and nose are at the center of the headpiece.

Pet Head   Show Head

The Face

1 With thinning shears, clear the excessive hair at the inside corners of the eyes, but leave the longer fur in the stop area. There is a small cowlick just above the inside corners of the eye. With thinning shears, lightly remove the coat from this cowlick, but leave all the longer hair over the brow. This will serve as a frame for the deep-set eyes.

2 Standing to the side of the dog, rest your hand gently at the top of the head, fingers toward the eye area. Comb all the hair from the sides of the face up to the top of the skull, from the eye area to the ears, catching the long coat between your fingers. Once all the hair is combed up and held firmly between your fingers, find the median line of the skull, or the center groove.

3 Draw the coat up directly above that line. With thinning shears, trim the coat to be level with the tops of the ear tips, trimming in a line just above your fingers.

When you release the coat, the hair will feather beautifully over the top part of the head. Repeat the process with the hair from the center point of the skull and the occiput.

4 With curved shears used in reverse, create a deep-set arch over the eyes to frame them. Buffer the line with thinning shears to soften it once the shape has been set.

❶ The Nose and Muzzle

Comb the fur in an outward and downward fashion over the nose. Neaten with thinning shears on a diagonal line that parallels the end of the muzzle, leaving at least an inch or two of hair.

❷ Looking from the side, comb the coat down over the muzzle and cheeks. Trim the lower jaw line to balance with the round headpiece, keeping the nose and eyes at the center of the circle.

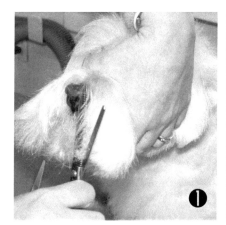 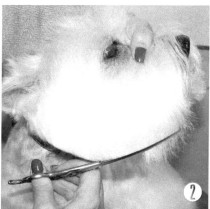

- Neaten the neck area with thinning shears so that the longer fur of the headpiece is even but very natural looking. Finish by reviewing the outline, combing all the hair up and out, allowing it to drop in a natural manner. Trim any long hair that falls outside the lines of a natural, neat head style with deep-set eyes.

Tips for Creating a Round Head on Harsh Coated Dogs

- Using the tip of the ear to establish the length of coat helps evenly shape the entire headpiece in a balanced manner.

- Removing the long hair in the cowlicks just above the eyes will aid in setting an even brow line.

- Using high quality thinning shears with the lay of hair will minimize sharp lines that are easily cut into the coat with standard shears.

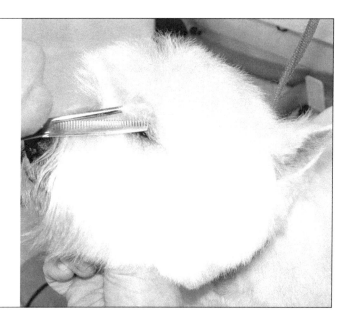

Tied Up Topknots

LETTING THE DOGS SEE THE WORLD

The topknot style is traditionally used on such long coated, drop coated breeds as the Shih Tzu or Maltese to keep their hair out of their eyes. In the pet world, tied up topknots are used on many breeds or mixed breeds with this coat type. The hair is effectively caught up onto the top of the head with small elastic bands.

SINGLE TIE-UP

On light coated dogs, hair can be pulled up into a single topknot and held in place with an elastic band. Start by thoroughly brushing the topknot coat. Mist it slightly with an anti-static spray to make it easier to pull smoothly together at the top of the head. Pull up a section of coat from the center part of the head and band it with a small elastic band. On dogs with moderate to heavy coats, single topknots stay in place better by combining two ponytails at the center of the headpiece. For the second ponytail, pull up the section just behind the eyes and gather it into the existing ponytail. If the coat is moderate, use another band to combine this section with the first ponytail. If the coat is really heavy, you may wish to band the second ponytail itself before combining it with the first ponytail using a third band.

Depending on the size and shape of the skull, you can use the eyes as a reference point to determine the amount of coat to gather into the band. On some dogs, the reference point will start at the center of the eye, others at the outer corners of the eyes. Once the coat is gathered into one topknot, slide a comb between the skull and the elastic band to ensure that only hair is caught up within the elastic and not skin.

Finish out the topknot by applying a small bow. Such multiple-banded topknots stay in place better because there is less coat being gathered into each ponytail.

TIPS FOR NATURAL EARS

Use thinning shears around the outer edges of the ear leather to retain the natural look of the ear.

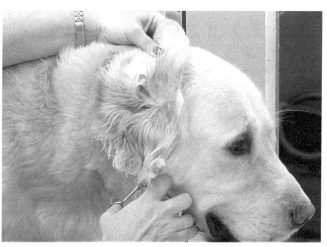

Lightly removing the longer heavy fur in front of the ear canal with thinning shears will aid in keeping it clean and cut down on odor.

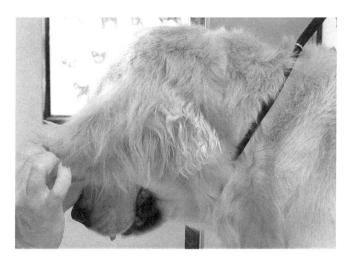

The small amount of soft downy undercoat that is long and wispy and commonly found at the base of the ear can easily be finger plucked to help neaten an outline.

Other breeds can also have excessively furry ears, especially heavily coated dogs, and grooming them "by the book" may not look right on the dog. Before making a significant styling change in the overall look of an ear, *always* consult the owner.

Beveled Ear Style

BALANCE WITH THE BREED PROFILE

This ear style is found on many dogs—such as the Poodle, Bichon or Shih Tzu—with dropped ears and long coats requiring full haircuts. The key with this ear is to keep it in style with the breed profile, as well as nicely balanced to suit the trim and body shape of the pet. Most beveled ears have a soft curve to their base or are left fully natural. The length can vary from being trimmed to the end of the ear leather or left well beyond.

No matter the ear length, the process is the same. Gently round the edge, giving it a nice curve or leave it blunt-cut with straight or curved shears. If the line is too sharp, soften it with thinning shears. Double-check the front and the back side of the bevel for smoothness.

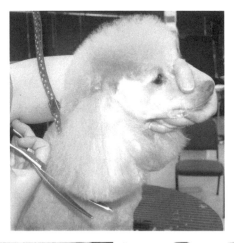

Dogs with longer ear furnishings often have a noticeable residue from being dragged in the food and water dish. Consult with the owner about trimming the ear length to the end of the nose to eliminate this problem. The length of the muzzle will determine the length of the ear furnishings.

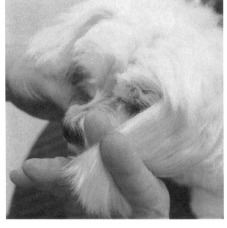

TIPS FOR BEVELED EARS

- The ear coat must be squeaky clean and totally mat and tangle free.

- To remove a fair amount of length, trim first with standard straight or curved shears.

- Double and triple check the shape of the bevel, especially on the inner back section of the ear.

- Afterward, if you want a softer look, edge lightly with thinning shears.

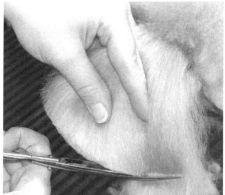

Make sure ears are even.

- Always be highly aware of the length and location of the ear leather prior to trimming.

- An ear leather that droops substantially longer than its mate is common on pets that have had a stroke.

Combination Ear Style

SPORTING DOGS SPECIAL

Many of the sporting dogs have this ear style. The top section is very short while the lower section is long and feathered.

TYPICAL BREEDS WITH THIS STYLE ARE:

Clumber Spaniel

Cocker Spaniel

English Setter

On some of the breeds—such as the Clumber Spaniel, the Sussex Spaniel, and the Irish Red and White Setter—the top of the ear is barely touched, especially if the dog is not carrying a lot of excessive feathering on the ear leather. Other breeds should have the top portion of their ears very cleanly clipped, fully exposing the top of the ear, as on the Cocker Spaniel. Variances will come into play on all breeds based on the amount of coat and the actual set of the ear.

Ear tops on lightly coated breeds often can be lightly trimmed with thinning shears to clear extra coat; other times, softly clearing the bulk of hair with a short clipper blade, such as a #10, will be acceptable. With either method, the look should be very subtle.

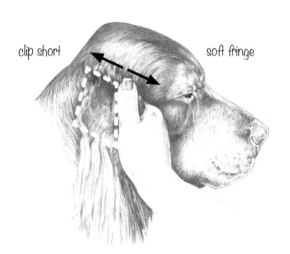

clip short   soft fringe

On some dogs with this ear style, like the English Setter and some Gordon Setters, you leave a soft fringe of coat at the front edge of the ear leather to softly frame the face. Think of cupping your hand at the top of the ear with your thumb at the front edge — the leather that just fits in the cup of your hand is left long and everything behind the hand is clipped short.

When clipping, continue to cup the front of the ear with your hand and use a #10 or #15 blade. Your hand will both shield the soft fringe from becoming accidentally caught in your clippers and prevent the dog from shaking it's head quickly.

① ② ❸ ④ ⑤

❶ On most other breeds, the top outside of the ears is trimmed close to the skin with clippers. Clip the top quarter to one-third of the ear leather on the outside of the ear with a #10 or #15 blade, either with or against the coat growth based on coat density and skin sensitivity.

❷ On the outside of the leather, the blending line will be a soft "U" shape. Keep this line above the widest section of the ear.

❸ On Cockers, English Cockers and English Springer Spaniels, clip the inside of the ear with a very close blade ranging from a #40 to a #10.

Use a light touch and clear the upper section inside the ear leather to assist with the sanitation and overall health of the ear. If ear problems are present, clip farther down on the inside of the ear leather to alleviate the problem.

❹ Edge the top front section of the ear leather with detailing shears, keeping the tips of the shears towards the tips of the ears. Do not edge past the point of the clipped sections on the outside of the ear leather. Setters normally do not have the inside or front of the ear leather trimmed unless they are very heavily coated or have an ear problem.

❺ Lightly round the long feathering at the bottom of the ears with shears for a neat, finished look.

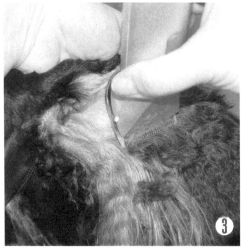
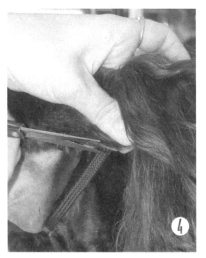
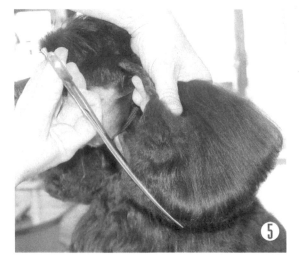

TIPS FOR THE COMBINATION EAR

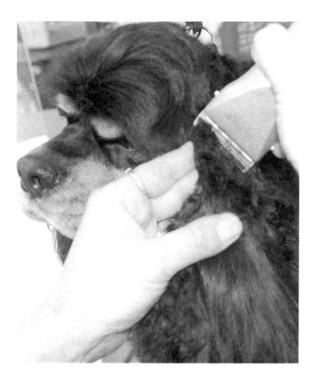

When trimming an ear with clippers, always work from the center of the leather out to the edge so the front of the ear leather does not get caught between the teeth of the blade.

The line at the top of the head where the ear leather meets the skull should be invisible.

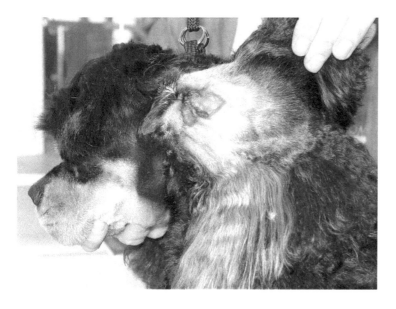

If there is a health concern with the ear canal, clip the inside of the ear closely to help keep it cleaner for the owner and minimize the weight of the ear. This allows for better air circulation that can aid healing.

Clipped Ear Style

NEATNESS IS THE KEY

We see clean, clipped ear styles on both cropped and uncropped ears in many breeds and mixed breeds. The entire ear leather on most breeds is clipped with the exception of the Soft Coated Wheaten, where the clipping only goes to the break or bend of the ear; and the Scottish Terrier, where an inner ear tuft is left at the inner base of the ear. A few pricked-eared breeds have just the tips of their ears clipped such as Yorkies or Westies. The key with any clipped ear is to work safely, clipping from the center of the ear leather out toward the edges. When edging the ears with shears, always use small detailing shears to minimize the risk of nicking the ear leather and keep the tips of the shears towards the tips of the ears. In the end, neatness is the key component of this ear style.

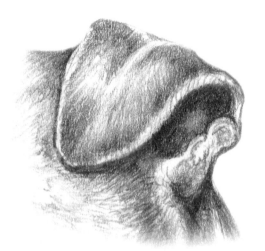

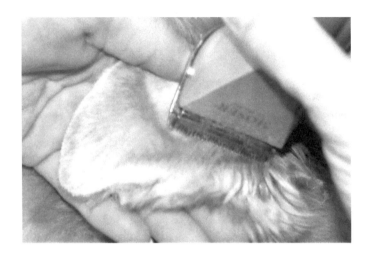

Most ears are clipped with a close blade. It is common to see a #10 or #15 blade used on the outside of the ear leather while a #40 blade is used on the inside. When working with close blades in this delicate area, always work from the base, or center, of the ear out toward the edge. Gently brace the ear with your fingers to clip over it. To finish, use small finishing shears to trim around the outside edge of the ear leather, keeping the tips of the shears toward the tip of the ear.

Think of an ear like a leaf on a tree — they all have veins starting from the leaf stem. The veins go down the center of the leaf working their way to the outer edges of the leaf. When you clip an ear, think of it like a leaf. Follow the veins in the leaf when clipping.

With some dogs, leaving the outside of the ear leather a bit longer is common such as on the Soft Coated Wheaten or pet dogs where a teddy bear ear is created with a #7F or longer blade. Longer blades—beyond a #15 blade—can create serious safety issues if extreme care is not used. The smaller the dog, the larger the risk of nicking an ear leather with the blade. Done carefully, with a dog that cooperates for grooming, the risk is slight. Some dogs look better with fuller ears that result from a #7F, up to being skimmed with an attach-on guard comb. As with the closer ear, work from the center out, bracing the backside of the ear. Edge the ear using small shears, keeping the tips of the shears toward the tip of the ear.

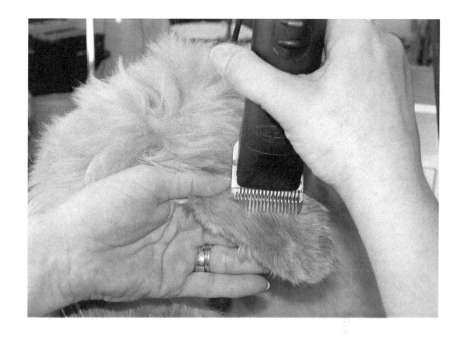

TIPS FOR CLIPPED EARS

Always clip from the center of the ear to the outer edges.

❶ On the inside of the ear, watch for the small flap of skin near the base of the ear where the ear and neck connect.

❷ Always use small detailing shears near the edge of an ear and support the ear leather between your fingers as you trim.

❸ Keep the tips of the shears towards the tip of the ear. Whether it is a cropped or natural ear carriage.

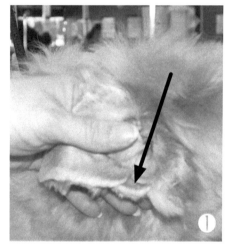

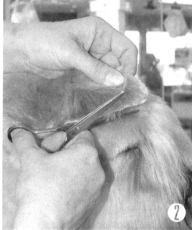

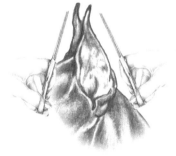

Tasseled Ears

A COMBINATION OF THE CLIPPED EAR & THE COMBO EAR

This is not the most common ear style, but we do see it on a such breeds as the Bedlington Terrier and the Dandie Dinmont. It's also a style that can be done on any pet with fully feathered ears such as Poodles, Shih Tzus and many mixed breeds styles. It's a combination of the clipped ear and the combo ear style.

Typical Dogs with this Style are:

Bedlington Terrier

Dandie Dinmont

Shih Tzu

Poodle

Pumi

Mixed Breeds

The key difference between the combo ear and the tasseled ear is how far down the ear leather is trimmed. The tasseled ear is clipped beyond the widest point of the ear. Coat is only left on the lower portion of the ear leather. As with the clipped ear, a shorter blade is preferred, such as a #10 or #15 on the outside of the ear and a #40 on the inside. The outer edge needs to be detailed with small detailing shears, again keeping the tips of the shears towards the tip of the ear.

Tasseled Ear   Combo Ear

TIPS FOR THE TASSELED EAR

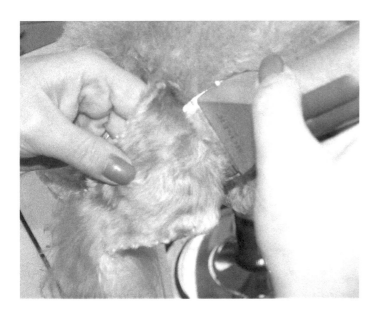

Work from the center of the ear leather to the outer edges. Bracing the ear from the back enhances the smoothness and safety factor.

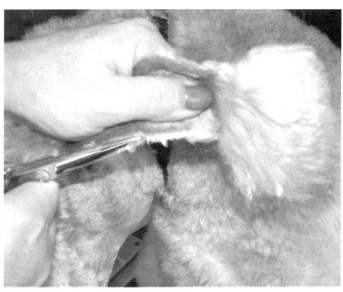

Always edge the clipped areas with small detailing shears, keeping the tips of the ears towards the tip of the ear.

Note: On the inside of the ear, watch for the small flap of skin near the base of the ear where the ear and neck connect.

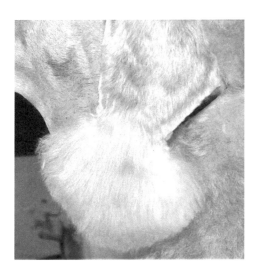

Clipped sections should be neat and clean.

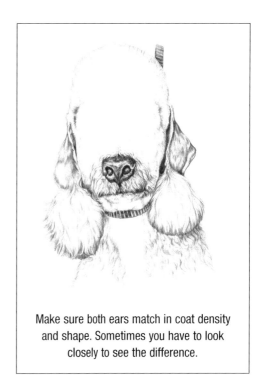

Make sure both ears match in coat density and shape. Sometimes you have to look closely to see the difference.

HOW MANY BASIC FEET STYLES ARE THERE?

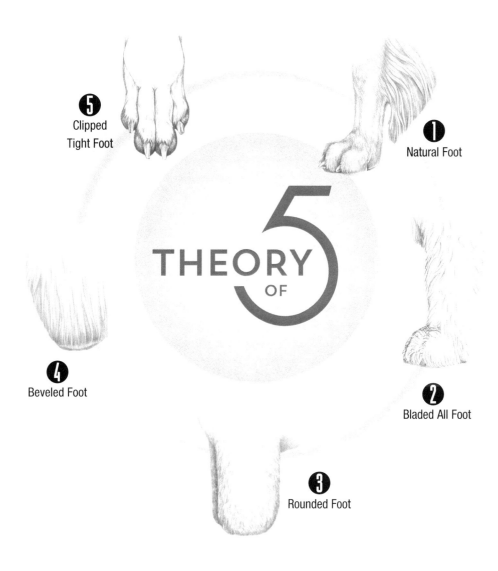

5 Clipped Tight Foot

1 Natural Foot

2 Bladed All Foot

3 Rounded Foot

4 Beveled Foot

THEORY OF 5

Natural Foot Style

TWO WAYS TO ACHIEVE: BY HAND OR WITH CLIPPERS

A groomer does not have to do anything to create this foot style on such dogs as the smooth coated and short coated types like the Dalmatian or Doberman.

With breeds that have longer coat, we need to trim the foot to make it look short, clean and natural. This is a very common practice with standard bath and brush pets such as Golden Retrievers, Shetland Sheepdogs, Newfoundlands and other moderate to longer coated dogs. There are two ways to trim the feet on most dogs—by hand or with clippers.

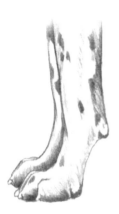

TRIMMING FOOT AND HOCK BY HAND

Trimming Technique #1

1 Once the pads are clean—with blades ranging from a #40 to a #15—move to the top of the foot. Hold the foot in your hand and back brush with a slicker brush, starting at the nail bed of the toes. Repeat the back brushing stroke three or four times to pull the long fur up from between the toes. Use the full pad of a firm slicker brush.

2 Once the coat is standing away from the foot, begin trimming with either thinning shears or small scissors. Hold the shears at right angles to the foot and cut straight up. Trimming in this manner will ensure a "well-arched toe."

3 Once the long fur is removed, lift your elbow so the shear runs parallel to the dog's leg. Lifting your elbow minimizes the risk of taking too much coat off the top of the knuckles and flattening the foot. Trim the long fur on the foot to the same length as the natural shorter coat found further up the leg, in the saddled area. When you finish, the foot should look very neat, as if it naturally grew that way. Thinning shears are a great help in achieving a natural finish on any coat type.

4 Do some light detailing around the nail bed of the foot with small detailing shears and/or thinning shears to get a really finished look.

5 Double-check the trimming work one last time by back brushing each foot. Trim any long strays found on the final brush-up.

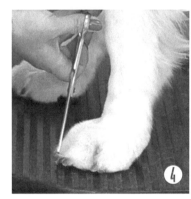

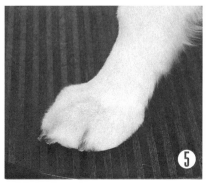

TRIMMING FOOT & HOCK BY HAND
Trimming Technique #1

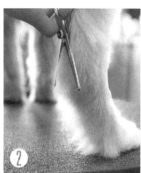
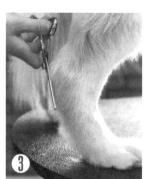

Hock

Hocks should appear neat and tidy on most breeds. They can be trimmed and detailed with either regular or blending shears. On pets, the result should look natural, accentuating the dog's structure.

❶ Brush coat to one side of the hock.

❷ Trim off any longer coat falling outside the line of the leg with shears, blenders or thinners.

Repeat on the opposite side of the hock.

❸ Brush coat back and trim off any uneven longer coat to accentuate the bone of the dog while keeping it looking very natural.

TIPS FOR TRIMMING THE NATURAL FOOT

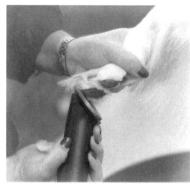

- Work with thinning shears or smaller shears around the foot to minimize the risk of cutting the foot or pad.

- A # 40 blade used on the pads reduces the risk of cutting a pad and can be used for both trimming and edging the foot.

- Trimming the feet on a clean dog will maximize the sharp edge of blades or shears.

- When trimming by hand, make sure to get all the long hairs up from between the toes. There's nothing worse than sending the pet home only to have its owner discover stray long sprigs popping out.

Cutting through dirty fur is like using your good tools to cut through sandpaper.

There are two ways to shape this foot style, the long way by hand or the quick way with clippers. Shaping the foot by hand allows a stylist to correct conformational flaws with ease. It takes a little longer, but for a talented stylist, this method ensures a quality unavailable with the short cut. However, there are tricks to getting the rounded foot shape quickly and easily by following a few simple rules. The quicker way to rough in a round foot is with clippers while you are trimming the pads. For the everyday pet, this technique offers a nice, fast, safe way to trim feet, but the ability to correct conformational faults is lost.

Trimming Technique #1

1 When shaping the foot by hand, first clean the pad of long hair with blades ranging from a #40 to #15. The foot is then blocked in with straight lines to create a square box. Brush/comb the foot thoroughly with a heavy slicker or comb to eliminate any tangles and fluff the coat. Make sure the dog is standing squarely on the table. The initial trim line should be straight across the front two digits of the foot or where they should be pointing if the dog was conformationally correct. The following two cuts should be along the outside edges. The final cut should be along the rear of the foot, completing the box.

2 Straight shears are used for this process. To set up this technique correctly, the bottom blade of the shear glides along the tabletop next to the dog's foot as the pet stands in a natural position. The shear needs to be beveled up and away from the pad of the foot.

3 Once the foot is boxed in, go back with curved shears and take off the corners of the box.

4 Next, pick the foot up—either under the elbow or above the hock—and brush the coat down over the foot. Check and reshape the foot if there is not a smooth, soft "U" shape. Make sure to view the foot from the top and *only* cut at the edges, *never* under the foot from top view. Re-brush the foot and turn it over to check for long strays next to the pad. With small, detail shears, trim anything that falls outside the guidelines you have already established. Shake the foot once more and place it on the table. The shape should be full, round and neat.

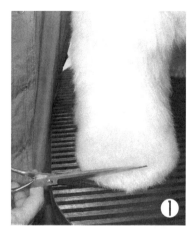

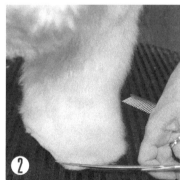

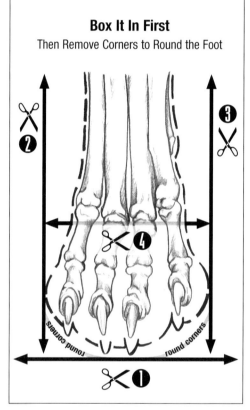

Box It In First
Then Remove Corners to Round the Foot

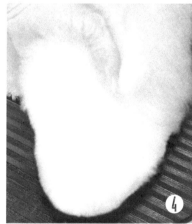

Trimming Technique #2

The faster method is to set the basic shape of the round foot with clippers at the same time you are clipping the pads with blades ranging from a #40 blade to a #15.

❶ Brush the foot area thoroughly with a heavy slicker brush to eliminate all tangles. When the brush glides easily through the hair, brush all the fur down over the foot.

❷ Next, slide your hand down the dog's leg, thumb toward the table and pick up the foot.

❸ First, gently clip out the pad. Using your hand and fingers as a brace, clip off the excess hair hanging beyond the outside edge of the foot. Keep the blade level with the foot pad. Do not cut up into the side coat of the foot.

❹ To make the feet appear neatly rounded and forward facing, you will need to finish them off with shears while the dog stands naturally on the table.

Soften the line with thinning shears, if desired. This technique allows you to both trim the pads and roughly round the foot, all in one motion. This method is better for dogs with small to moderate feet and should not be used on dogs that have extremely poor fronts or extremely large feet.

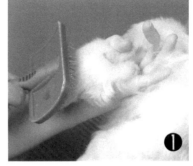
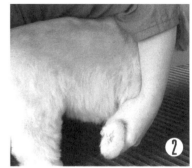

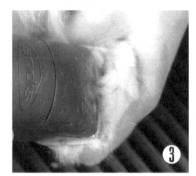

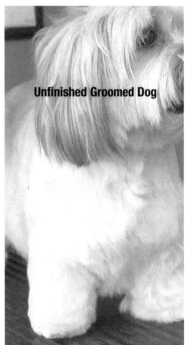

Unfinished Groomed Dog

Finished Foot.

TIPS FOR SHAPING THE ROUND FOOT

- The coat must be exceptionally clean and fluff dried as straight as possible.

- Use a heavy slicker brush to pull the coat down over the foot so that each hair shaft is in line with its neighbors. The operation is similar to a hairdresser who combs all the hair in one direction, holding the hair between the fingers, then trimming the ends.

- Double- and triple-check your work before the pet leaves the table.

- When working on the pads with scissors when the foot is picked up, only use small detail shears less than 6" long to minimize the risk of cutting them.

- When rounding the foot by hand, box it in first to eliminate the "pointed toe" look.

- When rounding the foot with scissors, open the blades, gliding them through the fur to be trimmed. The bottom blade of the shear will glide along the table top. Keep the shear close to the foot but beveled outward eliminating the risk of cutting the foot.

Setting in a round foot with a clipper *does not* work well with exceptionally large feet, heavy coats or on dogs that are poorly built when standing square.

The Beveled Foot

GETTING IT NEAT & TIDY

Bevels on such full coated dogs as the Cocker or Lhasa Apso can be a challenge to get neat and tidy. The heavier the coat, the bigger the challenge. Keys to having the bevel come out well are based on sound coat prep before the trimming, the thoroughness of the combing while trimming bevels and the sharpness of your shears.

The goal with this foot style is consistent feet in shape and size. The bevels should flow smoothly into the undercarriage of the dog, almost creating a seamless flowing line. The upper edge of the bevel is at the discretion of the stylist, however, it needs to be consistent on all four feet.

Untrimmed   Trimmed

Trim the pads with a close cutting blade ranging from a #15 to a #40. Use a very light touch to clean the pads of long hair. Thoroughly line comb and brush every section of the feathering. Once the coat is free of mats and tangles, you can shape the feet into round, beveled circles or begin to neatly shape the outline of the undercarriage line.

On lighter coated dogs, start with the dog standing squarely on the table, comb all the fur straight down over the foot. Begin trimming a foot by forming a box around it with long straight shears. Bevel the shears so there will be an upward curve from the foot to the outer line of the coat. Once you have a box, re-comb the fur and with long, curved shears, begin forming the round, beveled foot. Blend the bevels of the feet into the undercarriage line so it creates one continuous line.

1 For heavier coated dogs with coat all one length, begin by thoroughly combing the coat down while the dog stands squarely on the table.

2 Begin to outline the shape of the flowing undercarriage line starting at the center of the dog, work outward towards the rear and front of the dog. Let your shears glide along the tabletop to start setting the line.

3 Once the outline is established, lift and separate a section of coat from around each foot, allowing for a clearer view of the foot. Pick the foot up and lightly scissor around the edge of the foot. Set the foot back down, recomb the coat.

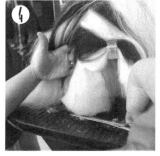

4 Box in each foot first, then round and edge the foot. Drop the longer fur back into place and re-comb the coat. Check your line and re-trim if necessary. Repeat on all four feet.

5 Once the basic shape of the undercarriage is created, then create the beveled edge with curved shears, allowing the coat to clear the ground while adding neatness and flair to the overall outline.

TIPS FOR TRIMMING BEVELS

- Comb. Comb. Comb

- Make sure the dog is standing up and square on the table while trimming the bevels.

- Use long shears to start the shape. Once the basic shape is cut in, change to a shear that matches the size of the dog.

- On really heavy coated dogs, once the basic foot shape is created, slide your fingers between the toe digits, pulling longer coat through to the foot pad. Re-comb and fluff top of the foot. Trim the longer hair from between the digits level with the foot pad.

- Use an anti-static spray if the coat is fly-away.

Poodle Feet

A CLEAN FOOT IS THE KEY

These feet are the most tedious and difficult to learn. However, if you don't get close, the feet turn out sloppy.

Many stylists also have a difficult time trimming the foot in a timely fashion. A proficient stylist should be able to complete all four feet in 3–6 minutes for small- to medium-sized dogs. Working on a clean foot will extend the life of your blade and make it easier to clip the foot.

Trimming Technique

- For a clipped foot, the feet are clipped totally clean. The digits of the foot are clipped to a point where the bones of the feet meet the metacarpals and metatarsal bones or the bones of the pasterns. There is a slight bump on the sides of the foot where these bones join.

❶ On pets, use a close blade like a #15 blade, in reverse, with a light touch. Start by clipping the top of the two center digits. Start at the nail bed. Tip the blade up so only the front edge of the blade contacts the skin. The effective movement of the clipper is a soft, push-push as you clear the hair from the foot. The strokes are a very short forward-and-back motion. Clear the hair to the point where the bones converge and there is a natural bend at the foot and the wrist.

❷ Proceed to the outside digits and repeat the process. Once the top of the foot is cleared, place your fingers on the underside of the foot and spread the toes. Glide just the edge of the blade in between the toes, using your fingers as buffers. Your fingers will protect the webbing between the toes from getting caught between the teeth of the clipper blade.

❸ Again, start at the nail bed and scoop out the long fur between the toes. Do one side of *all* the toes first, *then* rotate your clipper in and repeat the procedure on the other side of *all* the toes.

When finished, double-check your work for long strays. Trim the pads with a close blade ranging from a #15 to a #40. Use a very light touch to clean the pads of long hair.

Clipper Cuff Line

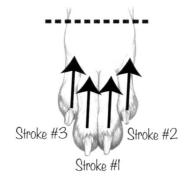

Stroke #3   Stroke #2

Stroke #1

For clipped foot styles use a close blade such as a #15 in reverse to clip the foot. Clip up the center two digits first—then clipper the outside toes. Start at the nail bed and trim up to the bulge at the side of the foot.

❶

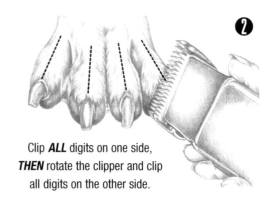

❷

Clip **ALL** digits on one side, **THEN** rotate the clipper and clip all digits on the other side.

Clean Up Around the Nail Bed

❶ There are a couple of ways to do this. One option is to simply turn the clipper over and touch the nail bed with the upside down #15 or #10 blade, using a very short, push motion.

❷ Another technique is to lightly edge the nail beds with a #40 blade after the toes have been clipped.

 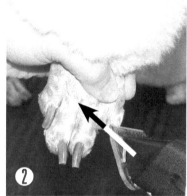

Finished Poodle Foot

Catching webbing between the digits with the clipper blade is very easy to do, causing discomfort for the pet. Use your fingers as protective buffers.

FOOT STYLES: POODLE FOOT

TIPS FOR CLIPPING A CLEAN FOOT

- Work with a clean dog.

- For most pets, use a #15 blade on the top of the foot, a #40 for the pads.

- If the pet has very light or soft skin, think about going at least one blade length longer on the top of the foot or work with the grain. Trim quality will be sacrificed but the dog will not be injured by clipper irritation.

- If the pet struggles with having its feet worked on, double-check your technique to ensure the webbing isn't getting nicked by the blade.

- With your fingers, push up the webbing from under the foot to ensure the area between the toes has been well trimmed.

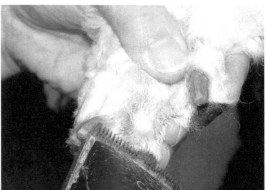

- If the pet pulls and you are not injuring it, hold the digits firmly by grasping the webbing between the center digits. This will give you a firm hold without hurting the pet. While holding the foot, place the heel of your hand on the table top, maintaining your grasp on the foot. Ignore the pet—as the pet struggles, he is uncomfortable—as he sits still, he's comfortable, immediately, giving positive and negative reinforcements. The dog will learn very quickly not to pull.

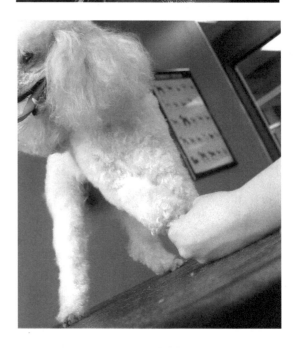

When trimming is required on a short, natural tail style, use the same blade that was used on the body. When trimming the underside of the tail, it may be necessary to change to a closer blade, like a #10 blade, to get around the rectum and to get the underside of the tail really neat.

Note: In some countries, tails are not docked as they are in the United States. Double check your country's styling trends for un-docked tails.

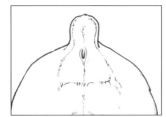

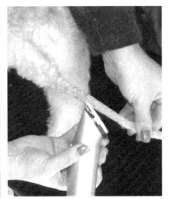

On "rat tails," only the end of the tail is trimmed very close to the skin. A #10 to #15 blade is routinely used to clip the last ⅔ to ½ of the tail. The blade can be used with or against the grain. The coat covering the base of the tail is hand-scissored short so that the two areas blend together seamlessly. The underside of the tail may be trimmed closer for sanitary reasons.

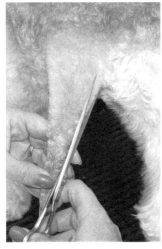
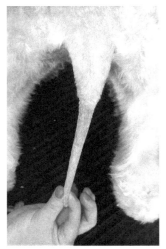

TIPS FOR CREATING A NATURAL TAIL

- When clipping a tail on a trimmed dog, make sure to double-check under the tail. Once the pet sees its owner, that tail will come up in a friendly wag, clearly exposing any sloppiness.

- Use a gentle touch when trimming under a tail and never let a blade come in contact with the rectum.

- Do not trim under the tail or around the rectum if it is already naturally short and neat.

The Flag Tail

REQUIRES A BIT OF SHAPING

We see this tail style on such breeds as the Golden Retriever, Setters and on many mixed breeds. To present a well balanced, neat outline, the tail normally requires a bit of shaping. The outline of the tail is a flag. With some breeds, like the English Setter, the shape is a clearly defined triangle. On other breeds, like on the Golden Retriever, the shape is softer in outline.

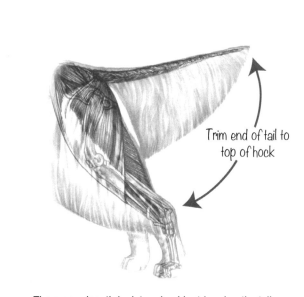

Trim end of tail to top of hock

The proper length is determined by trimming the tail tip even with the top of the hock. Once the length is established, then the shaping can start.

If a dog has an overabundance of tail coat, consult with the owners before any heavy trimming of this area.

1 Once the coat is mat and tangle free, brush all the tail coat down towards the ground in one direction. Trim the end with straight shears or thinners level with the hock.

2 Hold the tail out level with the body and begin trimming off with scissors the longer coat that falls outside of the triangular shape, broader at the base, tapering to a point at the tip.

With some breeds, this overall shape will be more angular than others.

With the overall shape established, soften the line to be a more natural styling outline with thinning shears or by cutting small "V"-shaped nips into the coat with straight shears. These "V"-shaped nips are shown in more detail on the next spread's plume tail.

3 Once the shape has been established on the "flag," turn your attention to the top line of the tail. If there is a bulge on the top of the tail close to the base, bulk thin the excess with thinning shears to make it lie flat.

4 There should be a break in the longer furnishings at the base of the tail and the rear of the dog. To form a clear but natural break at this point, lightly thin the bulk at the underside of the tail closest to the body. Less is more, so go easy with this trimming technique. When finished, the coat should look like it grew that way naturally.

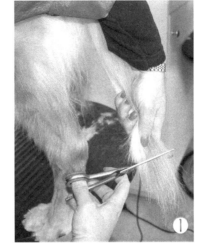

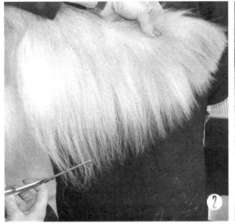

TIPS FOR CREATING A FLAG TAIL

- The tail must be clean, properly fluffed and brushed out.

- To create the proper balanced look, the length of tail is trimmed to the length of the hock.

- For some owners, a long flowing tail on their pet is a thing of great pride.

The Plume Tail

A LONGER MORE NATURAL LOOKING TAIL

This tail style is naturally long on many breeds such as the Shih Tzu, Maltese and Bichon. The plume may be left in its long and natural state, though some owners prefer to have it shortened. Even on the shortened tail, the stylist should simulate the look of the longer, natural tail. A variation of the plumed tail is the "lion tail." We see this on a few breeds, such as the Chinese Crested, the Löwchen and the Portuguese Water Dog.

Maltese: Long and Natural Plume Tail

Shih Tzu: Long and Natural Plume Tail

Löwchen: Lion Tail

Portuguese Water Dog

As shown in Step 1 of the flag tail, when a tail needs shortening, run your hand down the tail. Stop where you want to establish the length and trim off the excess hair beyond that point. Make the trim line slightly rounded in order to create a soft tip and not a hard straight line.

To create a natural looking plume tail, use thinning shears or straight shears to nip some "V"-shaped cuts into the fur, paralleling the strands of hair as they hang. The nips can be between 1" and 3" deep, depending on how much length needs to be removed. Use caution with this method if it is new to you. It takes time to perfect the technique.

Brush out the tail and hold it up over the back of the dog, mimicking the natural tail carriage, with the longer coat draping downward to check the shape and length of the tail.

A variation of the plumed tail is the lion tail. On most haircuts with this tail style, whatever blade was used on the body is continued down the tail. Half to two-thirds of the end of the tail should be covered with the plume. If the plume needs to be shortened, proceed in the manner outlined above.

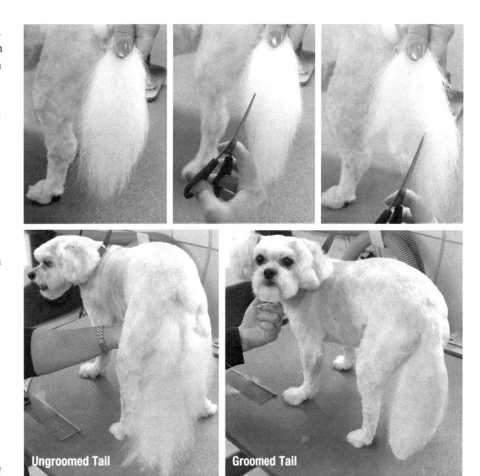

Ungroomed Tail

Groomed Tail

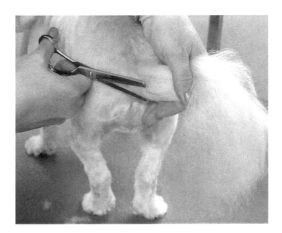

TIPS FOR SHAPING THE PLUME TAIL

- Make sure the tail is totally brushed out so that a fine-toothed comb can easily run through the entire tail.

- When shortening a plumed tail, make it look as natural as possible.

- If shortening the length with V nips, always hold your hand around the tail bone for protection.

- Double-check around the base of the tail for long strays or unevenness.

The Carrot Tail

A MOSTLY TERRIER TRAIT

This tail style is primarily a terrier trait, but we occasionally see it with other breeds or mixed breeds. The shape of the tail is wider at the base—tapering to a point at the tip. We see this tail style on West Highland White, Scottish and Cairn Terrier, as well as the Lagatto Romagnolo.

Cairn Terrier

Scottish Terrier

West Highland White Terrier

Lagatto Romagnolo

THEORY OF 5 — *Simplifying Pet Grooming Concepts for Everyday Pets ©2018*

1. There will be more coat on the sides and top of the tail than on the underside. When trimming the sanitary area under the tail, continue about a half inch to an inch up the back side of the tail and leave the rest to do by hand.

2. Trim off all the excessive length at the tip by running your hand down the tail, thumb towards the tip and stopping when you can feel the end of the tail bone under your thumb. With your fingers protecting the tip of the tail, trim off the long fur.

3. Fluff the coat and shape the tail with straight shears, thicker at the base, tapering to the tip.

4. When the tail is held upright, there should be no dip right in front of the tail where it meets the body. The sides should blend smoothly into the rump. The back of the tail is trimmed close, but not so close so that it is bald. Use thinning shears or a #7F in this area. Once the basic shape is established, soften the finish with thinning shears to give a natural look.

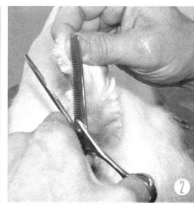

The completed tail shape looks like a thick carrot, wider at the base—tapering to the tip.

TIPS FOR SHAPING THE CARROT TAIL

- When cutting the excessive fur from the tip of the tail, always protect the tail bone by holding it in your fingers.

- There is never any excessive length or flag hanging off the back side of the tail.

- If there is an abundance of hair, start setting the basic shape with straight shears and then finish with thinning shears for a more natural look.

- When double-checking the shape, back comb the fur from the tip of the tail to the base.

The Pom-Pom Tail

COMMON WITH POODLES

This tail style is common with Poodles and Poodle mixes. A rounded tuft of fur is left at the end of the tail. If the pet has a beautiful, full coat and a long enough tail bone, the tail can be highly stylized. On pets that are lacking in these areas, a rounded tuft can still be created at the end of the tail.

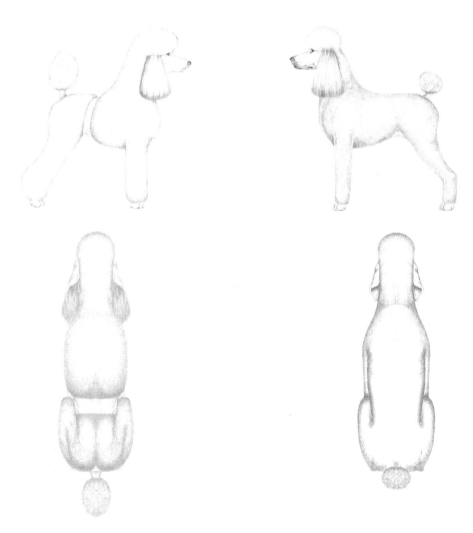

The pom-pom tail is clipped at the base, leaving a fuller shape on the end. When complete, the ratio of clipped tail to pom-pom should look balanced—regardless of the length of each individual dog's tail. The recommended ratios are applied to each dog's tail length. On dogs with extremely short or non-existent tail structures, it is appropriate to leave only the puff of fur, forming a "bunny tail."

To form a pom-pom tail, clip ¼ to ⅓ of the base of the tail bone with a #10 or #15 blade in reverse. Continue clipping around the base of the tail to the point where it meets the body. Clip a small inverted "V" at the top of the tail, in line with the spine. When the dog raises its tail, this indentation will eliminate the small bump of hair that is common when the clipped line is not carried up far enough. On shorter coated trims, this line will be very minor compared with longer hand-scissored haircut styles where an exaggerated "V"-shape can add style and flair to the trim. The pom-pom is created by hand-scissor the remaining ¾ to ⅔ of the tail into a ball or oval shape — depending on what shape the owner has requested or looks best on the dog.

On some tails, the bone may be so short or non-existent that only a puff of fur can be left, hence the "bunny tail."

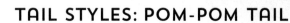

① ② ③ ④ ⑤

❶ For highly stylized trims, the tip of the pom-pom should be almost in line with the top of the skull.

❷ For pet trimming, this is normally scaled back a bit. Start by combing all the fur to the end of the tail. Twist the fur that extends beyond the bone between your fingers.

❸ While holding the firmly twisted fur, hold the tail up in a natural position. Trim to the desired length. Trimming the end of the tail in this fashion creates a bevel.

❹ Once the end has been trimmed, hold the tail up and out by grasping a small section of hair, holding it between two fingers. Comb all the fur down towards the body and bevel the coat that falls below the clipped line on the tail bone.

❺ Re-fluff the coat and shape the center, creating either a round ball or an oval shape.

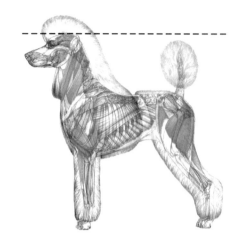

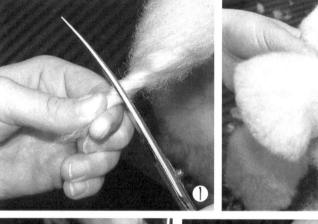

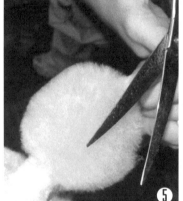

Finished Pet Tail

TIPS FOR SHAPING THE POM-POM TAIL

- On pets that have a longer tail bone, the pom-pom shape will be more oval, especially is the tail is left in it's natural, undocked state.

- The shape will be more ball-like on pets that lack length in the tail bone.

- When beveling the lower line of the pom-pom, comb the coat down and trim well below the clipped line.

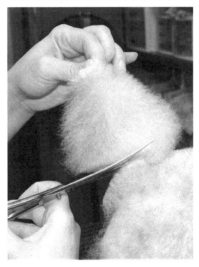

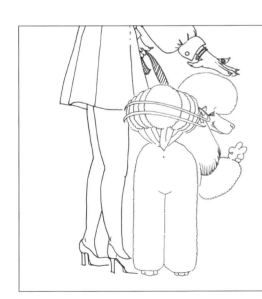

If time becomes an issue in a busy grooming salon, this is the area where you can save time by not being overly picky, but make sure the tail is neat. Once the owner picks up the dog, the tail is in constant motion or the dog is sitting on it.

IN CONCLUSION

The core concept of the *Theory of 5* is simplicity. There is nothing complex or magical about the process. Success depends upon the ability of the professional pet stylist to safely and humanely handle all pets. Key to that success is repeatability—the application of high quality work for each and every size and breed of pet. By applying the concepts described in these pages, consistent trimming skills can easily be mastered—helping bring success to your doorstep and well-trimmed, graciously styled pets to the community.

The pets that were photographed for this book are the typical pet dogs we see every day at our salons. No "conformation show dogs" were used. The typical family pets that walk through your salon or mobile grooming van doors are no less important to their owners than any high-profile show dog and deserve no less than your best effort.

The *Theory of 5* concept has brought a high level of success to my businesses over the years and I hope it will to yours as well.

Happy Trimming!

Melissa Verplank

ABOUT MELISSA VERPLANK

Melissa Verplank & "White Dogs" Cache and Pearl

Melissa Verplank began her pet grooming career in 1979. Her mastery of grooming techniques won her numerous awards on a national and international level.

During her formative years, she ran a fleet of mobile grooming units and a busy grooming salon. Drawn to teaching, in 1991 Verplank founded The Paragon School of Pet Grooming Inc. which is recognized as a top training facility. With the rise of distance learning, Verplank launched Learn2GroomDogs.com in 2010, an on-line streaming video library of educational material for all levels of professional pet grooming and styling.

Ms. Verplank is an award-winning author of multiple pet educational products—including books, videos and training programs. Verplank has been a member of GroomTeam USA, was the GroomTeam USA Coordinator and currently sits on the Board. She is an industry speaker, contest grooming judge, the recipient of Pet Age's Industry Icon Award, and multiple-time Cardinal Crystal Achievement and Barkleigh Honors award winner.

Ms. Verplank and her husband reside on a farm in West Michigan where they share their lives with Maremma Sheepdogs, multiple felines, chickens, and horses — both Friesians and Rocky Mountains.

Education is not the filling of a pail, but the lighting of a fire.

William Butler Yeats

The word paragon means "in search of excellence" and this search is the driving force behind the Paragon School of Pet Grooming curriculum. Melissa Verplank, President and Owner, has personally developed the training programs. She has gone to great lengths to ensure thoroughness and relevance at all stages of a student's development. Ms. Verplank works tirelessly to stay on the leading edge of the grooming industry by being an international judge, speaker, author and advocate for the pet industry.

We are extremely proud of the caliber of our Trainers who provide individualized attention to each student. Students can enroll at our Michigan training center for hands-on instruction or complete online learning from Paragon through our Distance Learning Program (DLP). Our DLP is also a great way for salons to train new groomers fast with lots of additional coaching. Always an education leader, ongoing stand-out continuing education is available through our robust streaming video membership library—Learn2GroomDogs.com—all taught by talented industry leaders. Whichever method fits your life, learn with us!

EDUCATION PROGRAMS

Paragon is headquartered in Grand Rapids, Michigan and an Internationally Recognized Education Leader

616-667-7297 | paragonpetschool.com

ON CAMPUS TRAINING

All Breed Styling Program (600 hours)
This is our most popular training program for a person just beginning in the pet grooming industry. Upon successful completion of this program, the student will possess the necessary skills to launch their career in the grooming industry!

Basic Pet Styling Program (240 hours)
This program is a great option for students who may already be employed by a grooming salon or have practice pets outside of the Paragon School environment. This program is popular for salon owners or managers to enroll their newer team members in to develop their next level of grooming skills. This is a perfect salon, student, school partnership!

Basic Bather/Brusher Program (80 hours)
Learn the basic, groundwork fundamentals used everyday in a busy salon including proper pet handling skills, bathing and drying techniques, brushing and de-shedding, nail trimming and minor finish trimming on basic grooming pets. Many start here to determine if this industry is right for them; most continue because they love it!

DISTANCE LEARNING

Online Learning
Wish you could come to the Paragon School of Pet Grooming, but traveling to Jenison, Michigan is not an option? Then the Paragon School of Pet Grooming Distance Learning Program is perfect for you! As one of the only online programs rooted in and supported by a successful physical grooming school, the Distance Learning program offers a remote classroom experience using your computer or mobile device, complete with course guides, video, and personal evaluation and coaching from our team of instructors!

Learn2GroomDogs.com
This incredibly unique and extensive library of videos is at available to you for a small subscription price. The tutorials in this library span multiple breeds, trims, and techniques all proving to be a perfect tool to expand your skills to new heights! Our Training Partners have a minimum distinction of Certified Master Groomer. Many of whom are are award winning competitors, judges, and industry icons. Coupled with business topics, these videos are a must for any groomer looking to have a competitive edge over your competition!

CREATING EDUCATIONAL MATERIALS FOR THE PROFESSIONAL PET STYLIST.

whitedogenterprises.com

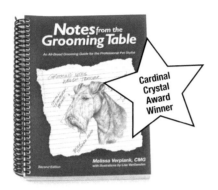

Cardinal Crystal Award Winner

Notes from the Grooming Table

An All Breed Guide for the Professional Pet Groomer and Stylist Second Edition 2016

613 pages; spiral bound 8.5" x 11"

Simply put, there is no book like this on the market. Melissa Verplank has teamed up with nationally recognized wildlife artist, Lisa VanSweden, to create this comprehensive grooming guide. The focus of *Notes* is basic pet trimming using typical pet grooming techniques. The illustrations are clear, concise and up-to-date for pet grooming styles and it features more than 200 breed profiles. Included are step-by-step instructions and hundreds of detailed illustrations to help you groom any breed of dog at a glance.

Shortcuts Reference Cards

Laminated; 11" x 8.5"
Complete Set (9 breeds)

Fully protected by heavy laminate Great for quick reference on many of the most popular and common pet grooming styles, including the Doodle, and as a useful visual aid during client consultations.

Notes Pocket Pal

101 pages; spiral bound 6.5" x 5" — fits about anywhere!

A perfect supplement to *Notes from the Grooming Table, Second Edition* this handy pocket-sized guide includes fully illustrated trim styles and easy-to-follow instructions for more than 40 groomable breeds — including drop coats.

Whiskers: Bow Making Made Simple!

32 page illustrated booklet

No matter how beautifully groomed it may be, a pet will attract attention much faster if it is sporting a bit of bright color. Applying bows or bandannas as a finishing touch on a fabulous groom is a sure way to generate interest—the *Whiskers Learning Journal* will show you how to create these fabulous bows with simple, clear step-by-step instructions.